S

D0404280

# ASHLAND & SOUTHERN OREGON

JUDY JEWELL & W. C. McRAE

# Contents

# ASHLAND AND SOUTHERN OREGON

When Oregonians talk about southern Oregon, they usually mean the southwestern corner of the state, including the upper valleys of the Umpqua and Rogue Rivers, the spine of the southern Cascade Mountains, and east to Klamath Falls. The outstanding features of this region include world-class culture-fests at Ashland and Jacksonville, the biggest chunk of remaining wilderness on the Pacific coast, and more summer sun and heat than you expect to find in Oregon.

It also includes Crater Lake National Park, Oregon's only national park, one of the most spectacular natural wonders in the United States. Driving up the desert slopes to the rim and then glimpsing the lake's startlingly blue water ringed by rock cliffs for the first time is a magnificent experience. On repeat visits, you'll want to explore some of the remoter areas of the park, perhaps the strange obelisk-like hoodoos in the southeastern part of the park, or the Boundary Springs, where some of Crater Lake's water percolates out from the edge of the caldera to form the headwaters of the Rogue River.

And speaking of rivers, the Rogue and the Umpqua are dramatically beautiful, with abundant waterfalls, hair-raising rapids for rafters, and the best fishing in the state.

If you think of Oregon as a bastion of progressive politics, then some aspects of southern Oregon may surprise you. From back-to-the-land idealists to hard-core survivalists, southern Oregon attracts settlers of all stripes. Added to this eclectic mix are more than 100 high-tech companies (the "Silicon Orchard"), white-water rafters, anglers, and theater lovers who

# HIGHLIGHTS

**( Lithia Park:** Trails at this lovely park lead from the formal gardens through an arboretum to wild woodlands (page 5).

**( Oregon Shakespeare Festival:** Take in a show at one of the world's great theater festivals (page 11).

**( Table Rocks:** These mesas contain the most interesting and easily accessible hiking destination along the I-5 corridor (page 19).

**( Oregon Caves National Monument:** Here you'll find stalactites and stalagmites deep inside a mountain, plus the unexpected pleasure of a classic mountain lodge (page 38).

**( Wildlife Safari:** Oregon's only drive-through zoo features 600 animals from around the world, including lions, giraffes, and hippopotamuses (page 41).

**( North Umpqua Waterfalls:** The drive from Roseburg to Toketee Falls along the North Umpqua is dotted with stunning waterfalls (page 48).

**( Crater Lake National Park:** At the nation's deepest lake, caused by a catastrophic volcanic eruption 6,600 years ago, you won't believe the color of the water (page 59).

**( Favell Museum:** Admire the collection of Native American artifacts and the gallery of Western art at this fine Klamath Falls museum (page 65).

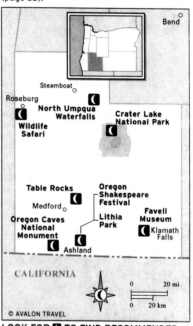

LOOK FOR **(** TO FIND RECOMMENDED SIGHTS, ACTIVITIES, DINING, AND LODGING.

flock to the Oregon Shakespeare Festival in Ashland and the Peter Britt Music Festival in Jacksonville. It's an unlikely blend of populations, but confounding expectations is just part of the mix in southern Oregon.

## PLANNING YOUR TIME

Ashland and the **Oregon Shakespeare Festival** are undeniably the largest tourist draw in southern Oregon, although to make the most of this world-class theater festival you'll need to make plans and reserve seats and lodgings well in advance. If you've waited until the last minute and can't get play tickets, you can sign up for a backstage tour of the festival, watch the free Green Show, and enjoy some of Ashland's fine restaurants—but even for these you'll need to have reservations if you want to eat early in the evening. Once the theater hordes leave the restaurants around 7:30pm, however, you can have your pick of the tables in Ashland's dining establishments.

Increasingly, southern Oregon is becoming a major center for wine production, and it's easy to add a bit of wine-tasting to your theater itinerary. We've included some of our favorite wineries, and for a full listing of area wineries, go to the **Southern Oregon Wineries Association website** (www.sorwa. org), where you can download a brochure and map.

Southern Oregon's other top destination is **Crater Lake National Park.** Even though a visit to the park itself—which for most travelers involves driving the loop route around the rim of the caldera—can be hectic due to excessive traffic, the approaches to the park along the Rogue or Umpqua river valleys offer excellent opportunities for less-thronged outdoor recreation.

The larger cities of southern Oregon— Medford, Grants Pass, and Roseburg—are mostly utilitarian with little to delay or seduce the traveler. If you were planning to camp during your Oregon visit, this might be the best place to do so.

# Ashland

Few towns are as closely identified with theater as Ashland (pop. 21,000). Tickets to the renowned Oregon Shakespeare Festival are the coin of the realm here, with contemporary classics and off-off-Broadway shows joining productions by the Bard. You can immediately sense that this is not just another timber town by the Tudor-style McDonald's, vintage Victorian houses, and high-end clothing stores on Main Street.

Blessed with a bucolic setting between the Siskiyous and the Cascades, Ashland embodies the spirit of the chautauqua movement of a century ago, which dedicated itself to bringing culture to the rural hinterlands. Until the 1930s, however, entertainment in these parts mostly consisted of traveling vaudeville shows that visited the Ashland-Jacksonville area to cheer up the residents of a gold rush community in decline.

Southern Oregon University, at the time named Ashland College, established the Shakespeare Festival in 1935 under the direction of Professor Angus Bowmer. Such noted thespians as George Peppard, Stacy Keach, and William Hurt graced Ashland's stages early in their careers, and the festival has garnered its share of Tony Awards and other accolades. Today, the Oregon Shakespeare Festival is the largest classic repertory theater in the country and enjoys the largest audience of any kind of theater in the United States. Annual attendance generally exceeds 400,000.

Ashland's tourist economy is also sustained by its auspicious location roughly equidistant to Portland and San Francisco. Closer to home, day trips to Crater Lake, Rogue River country, and the southern Oregon coast have joined the tradition of "stay four days, see four plays" as a major part of Ashland's appeal.

## SIGHTS
### ◖ Lithia Park

Ashland's centerpiece is 100-acre **Lithia Park** (340 S. Pioneer St.). Recognized as a National Historic Site, the park was designed by John McLaren, landscape architect of San Francisco's Golden Gate Park. It is set along Ashland Creek where the Takelma people camped and where Ashland, Ohio, immigrants built the region's first flour mill in 1854.

The park owes its existence to Jesse Winburne, who made a fortune from New York City subway advertising and in the 1920s tried to develop a spa around Ashland's Lithia Springs, which he said rivaled the venerated waters of Saratoga Springs, New York. Although the spa never caught on due to the Great Depression, Winburne was nevertheless instrumental in landscaping Lithia Park with one of the most varied collections of trees and shrubs of any park in the state. Winburne was also responsible for piping the famous Lithia water to the plaza fountains so all might enjoy its beneficial minerals. While many visitors find this slightly sulfurous, effervescent water a bit hard to swallow, many locals have acquired a taste for Ashland's acerbic answer to Perrier and happily chug it down.

A walk along the beautiful tree-shaded trail of **Winburne Way** is a must. This footpath and a scenic drive through the park start west of the Lithia Fountain. Redwoods, Port Orford cedars, and other species line the drive, which takes you along Ashland Creek to the base of the Siskiyou Mountains.

The hub of the park in the summer is the band shell, where concerts, ballets, and silent movies are shown. Children love to play at the playgrounds or feed the ducks in the ponds. Big kids enjoy tennis, volleyball, horseshoes, or exploring one of the many trails in the park, but dogs are not permitted in the park.

Pick up the *Woodland Trail* guide at the plaza's visitors center kiosk. The gentle milelong loop takes you from the plaza past a beautiful Japanese garden to the upper duck pond where mallards, wood ducks, and the endangered western pond turtle can be seen on the pond's island. A highlight for bird-watchers in winter is 100-200 wood ducks and ouzels diving for fish below the surface of Ashland Creek.

## Museums and Galleries

There are over 30 retail galleries in Ashland. Check out www.ashlandgalleries.com for an online guide and map. Two favorites are the **Hanson Howard Gallery** (89 Oak St., 541/488-2562, www.hansonhowardgallery. com, 10:30am-5:30pm Tues.-Sat.), which features monthly exhibits of contemporary artists in a bright airy shop next to the Standing Stone brewpub, and the **Gallerie Karon** (500 A St., 541/482-9008, 10:30am-5:30pm Tues.-Sat.), which features the works of 21 artists in an eclectic collection of sculpture, paintings, fiber arts, printmaking, photography, and jewelry. It is located in a thriving commercial strip by the railroad tracks.

**Schneider Museum of Art** (Southern Oregon University campus, 1250 Siskiyou Blvd., 541/482-6245, www.sou.edu/sma, 10am-4pm Mon.-Sat., $5 suggested donation) features contemporary art by national and

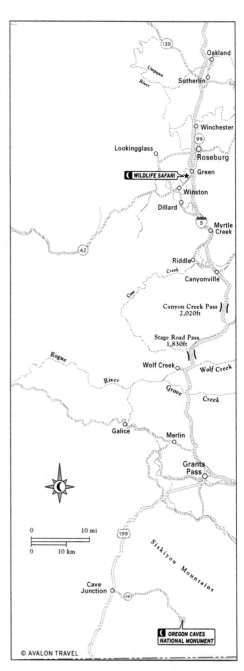

© AVALON TRAVEL

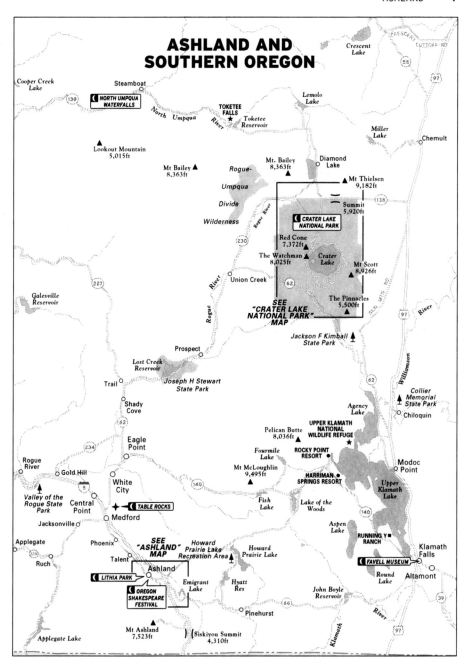

# ASHLAND AND SOUTHERN OREGON

Cooper Creek Lake

Steamboat

(138)

☾ **NORTH UMPQUA WATERFALLS**

Crescent Lake

CRESCENT CUTTOFF RD

(58)

(97)

North Umpqua River

**TOKETEE FALLS**
★ Toketee Reservoir

Lemolo Lake

Miller Lake

Chemult

▲ Lookout Mountain 5,015ft

Mt Bailey ▲ 8,363ft

*Rogue-*

Mt. Bailey 8,363ft

○ Diamond Lake

▲ Mt Thielsen 9,182ft

*Umpqua*

Rogue River

(138)

Summit 5,920ft

*Divide*

(230)

☾ **CRATER LAKE NATIONAL PARK**

*Wilderness*

Red Cone 7,372ft

The Watchman ▲ 8,025ft

Crater Lake

Mt Scott ▲ 8,926ft

○ Galesville Reservoir

(227)

Rogue River

Union Creek

(62)

The Pinnacles ▲ 5,500ft

Williamson River

(97)

**SEE "CRATER LAKE NATIONAL PARK" MAP**

Jackson F Kimball State Park ▲

Prospect

Lost Creek Reservoir

○ Trail

*Joseph H Stewart State Park*

(62)

Collier Memorial ♨ State Park

○ Chiloquin

○ Shady Cove

(62)

Agency Lake

(234)

Eagle Point

Pelican Butte ▲ 8,036ft

**UPPER KLAMATH NATIONAL WILDLIFE REFUGE** ★

Rogue River

○ Gold Hill

I-5

White City

Fourmile Lake

Mt McLoughlin ▲ 9,495ft

**ROCKY POINT RESORT** ●

Modoc ○ Point

*Valley of the Rogue State Park*

Central ○ Point

✦ ☾ **TABLE ROCKS**

(140)

**HARRIMAN SPRINGS RESORT** ●

*Upper Klamath Lake*

○ Jacksonville

○ Medford

Fish Lake

Lake of the Woods

(140)

○ Applegate

Phoenix ○

**SEE "ASHLAND" MAP**

*Howard Prairie Lake Recreation Area* ▲

*Howard Prairie Lake*

Aspen Lake

**RUNNING Y ■ RANCH**

Klamath Falls

○ Ruch

Talent ○

Ashland ○

Emigrant Lake

Hyatt Res

**FAVELL MUSEUM**

Round Lake

Altamont

☾ **LITHIA PARK**

☾ **OREGON SHAKESPEARE FESTIVAL**

John Boyle Reservoir

(66)

(39)

Mt Ashland ▲ 7,523ft

) 〔 Siskiyou Summit 4,310ft

○ Pinehurst

Klamath River

Klamath

(97)

*Applegate Lake*

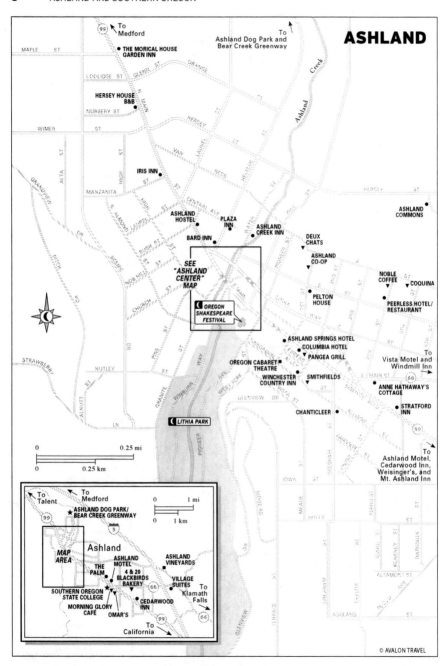

# ASHLAND

To Medford

To Ashland Dog Park and Bear Creek Greenway

MAPLE ST

THE MORICAL HOUSE GARDEN INN

COOLIDGE ST

GLENN ST

ORANGE

N MAIN

HERSEY HOUSE B&B

NURSERY ST

HERSEY

WIMER ST

Ashland Creek

ALTA

HIGH

VAN

LAUREL

NEES

HELMAN

HERSEY ST

GRANDVIEW DR

MANZANITA

IRIS INN

S ALMOND

LINCOLN

CENTRAL AVE

ASHLAND COMMONS

PITCH RD

NOB HILL

ASHLAND HOSTEL

PLAZA INN

ASHLAND CREEK INN

DEUX CHATS

BARD INN

SEE "ASHLAND CENTER" MAP

ASHLAND CO-OP

NOBLE COFFEE

COQUINA

CHURCH

PELTON HOUSE

PEERLESS HOTEL/ RESTAURANT

STRAWBERRY

PINE

OREGON SHAKESPEARE FESTIVAL

ASHLAND SPRINGS HOTEL

COLUMBIA HOTEL

PANGEA GRILL

To Vista Motel and Windmill Inn

NUTLEY

GRANITE

WINBURN WAY

WEST FORK

AVERY

OREGON CABARET THEATRE

WINCHESTER COUNTRY INN

SMITHFIELDS

E MAIN ST

66

ANNE HATHAWAY'S COTTAGE

ALNUTT

GLENVIEW DR

VISTA ST

CHANTICLEER

STRATFORD INN

LN

LITHIA PARK

PIONEER

FAIRVIEW ST

99

To Ashland Motel, Cedarwood Inn, Weisinger's, and Mt. Ashland Inn

0          0.25 mi
0          0.25 km

SISKIYOU

IOWA ST

MEADE

HOLLY

To Talent

To Medford

0          1 mi
0          1 km

ASHLAND DOG PARK/ BEAR CREEK GREENWAY

99

5

MAP AREA

Ashland

ASHLAND MOTEL

ASHLAND VINEYARDS

THE PALM

4 & 20 BLACKBIRDS BAKERY

66

VILLAGE SUITES

To Klamath Falls

SOUTHERN OREGON STATE COLLEGE

MORNING GLORY CAFÉ

CEDARWOOD INN

66

OMAR'S

To California

99

IDAHO ST

KEARNEY ST

HARRISON

ALTAMONT ST

TAYLOR

ASHLAND

GRAHAM ST

ABBOTT

TEMPLE

CLEVELAND

GLENDOWER

© AVALON TRAVEL

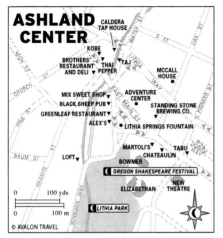

## ASHLAND CENTER

CALDERA TAP HOUSE

KOBE

BROTHERS' RESTAURANT AND DELI

THAI PEPPER

TAJ

MCCALL HOUSE

MIX SWEET SHOP

ADVENTURE CENTER

BLACK SHEEP PUB

STANDING STONE BREWING CO.

GREENLEAF RESTAURANT

ALEX'S

LITHIA SPRINGS FOUNTAIN

MARTOLI'S

TABU

CHATEAULIN

LOFT

BOWMER

OREGON SHAKESPEARE FESTIVAL

ELIZABETHAN

NEW THEATRE

LITHIA PARK

0    100 yds

0    100 m

© AVALON TRAVEL

international artists. Ashland is also home to the **ScienceWorks Hands-On Museum** (1500 Main St. near Walker St., 541/482-6767, www.scienceworksmuseum.org, 10am-5pm Wed.-Sat., noon-5pm Sun., $9 adults, $7 seniors and children ages 2-12, under age 2 free), a hands-on museum that offers interactive exhibits, live performances, and activities.

### Wine-Tasting

The climate of southern Oregon is ideal for many Bordeaux varietals such as cabernet sauvignon, sauvignon blanc, and merlot. Though the area's largest concentration of wineries is in the nearby Applegate Valley, a handful are close to Ashland.

Just east of town is **Weisinger's Vineyard** (3150 Siskiyou Blvd., 541/488-5989 or 800/551-9463, www.weisingers.com, 11am-5pm daily May-Sept., 11am-5pm Wed.-Sun. Oct.-Apr.). The vineyard, which has received national and international awards, produces cabernet sauvignon, viognier, pinot noir, chardonnay, sauvignon blanc, and Italian varietals.

## SPORTS AND RECREATION

**Ashland Mountain Supply** (31 N. Main St., 541/488-2749, 10am-6pm Mon.-Sat., 11am-5pm Sun.) rents outdoor recreation equipment at reasonable rates.

### Golf

A few miles outside of Ashland on Route 66 is **Oak Knoll Golf Course** (3070 Hwy. 66, 541/482-4311, www.oakknollgolf.org). Get into the swing of things before you play; at $16 for 9 holes and $24 for 18 holes, even if you triple bogey, you can't miss.

### Hiking

After the snow has melted, the walk to the top of **Mount Ashland** is an easy one with good views of the Siskiyou Mountains and 14,162-foot Mount Shasta in California. It's prudent to bring along a sweater even in warm weather, as it can get fairly windy.

The **Pacific Crest Trail** crosses the Mount Ashland road about three miles past the ski area. By early July, the snow is mostly gone and the wildflowers abundant.

### Horseback Riding

Saddle up and head out for a trail ride with **City Slickers** (776 W. Valley View Rd., 541/951-4611, www.oregontrailrides.com, $50 and up). A variety of rides in and around Ashland are available, and horses and guides are experienced with beginning riders.

### Mountain Biking

One of the more popular local bike rides is the **Lithia Loop Mountain Bike Route,** a strenuous 28-mile ride that gains 3,000 feet in elevation the first 6 miles. Caution is in order on the last 7 miles of descent. To avoid the steep ups and downs, you can drive up to the top and ride the fairly level 15-mile stretch. The Lithia Loop is mostly within the Ashland watershed, the source of the city's water supply, and it may be closed during midsummer and fall.

The **Siskiyou Crest Mountain Bike Route** begins at the Mount Ashland ski area parking lot. The 31-mile round-trip ranges from moderate to difficult and affords incredible views of Mount Shasta. The route ends at Dutchman Peak, where you'll find one of the few cupola-style fire lookouts left in the Pacific Northwest. This particular lookout was built in 1927. Note

© BILL MCRAE

The historic downtown core of Ashland is filled with fun places to shop and eat.

that bicycles are not allowed on the nearby Pacific Crest Trail.

The **Bear Creek Bike and Nature Trail** crisscrosses town before going down the valley to Medford along Bear Creek.

The **Ashland Ranger District** (645 Washington St., 541/482-3333) can provide directions and additional information about these and other mountain bike trails in the area.

## Skiing

Perched high atop the Siskiyou range and straddling the California-Oregon border is 7,523-foot **Mount Ashland** (541/482-2897, www.mtashland.com). To get here, take the Mount Ashland exit off I-5 and follow the road eight miles uphill.

While Mount Ashland is 15 miles from downtown Ashland by road, it's only eight miles away by Nordic ski trails. Skiers of all levels enjoy the 23 different runs, 100 miles of cross-country trails, and breathtaking vistas. The vertical drop here is 1,150 feet. An average of 325 inches of snow falls on the mountain, making it possible to ski from Thanksgiving through Easter. Daily lift rates are $36 weekdays, $43 weekends, and lower rates are available for seniors and youth (ages 7-17); children under seven ski free, and night skiing is $25. Don't forget to purchase your Oregon Sno-Park permit.

Spring and fall are good times to visit Ashland, as accommodation rates are lower than during the peak summer tourist season. Many proprietors include discounted Mount Ashland lift tickets with the price of the guest room.

## Water Sports

**Jackson WellSprings** (2253 Hwy. 99 N., 541/482-3776, www.jacksonwellsprings.com, $8 plus a once-yearly insurance charge of $3), a rather informal, decidedly hippie place, is 2 miles north of Ashland on the old highway and has a large naturally heated public swimming pool, a hot soaking pool, a sauna and steam room, as well as private mineral baths. The facility is open Tuesday to Sunday 8am-midnight June 15-Sept. 14; 9am-midnight April 15-June 14 and Sept. 15-Nov. 14; and noon-midnight Nov. 15-April 14. Clothing is optional in the evenings after 6pm. The pool is closed during the day on Monday but open after 6pm for "ladies night."

**Meyer Memorial Pool** (Hunter Park, Homes Ave. and Hunter Court, 541/488-0313, summer) includes a wading pool for infants and toddlers under age five as well as a large swimming pool for grown-ups.

Six miles east of Ashland on Route 66 is **Emigrant Reservoir** (541/776-7001). In addition to waterskiing, sailing, fishing, and swimming, there is a 270-foot twin flume waterslide (noon-6pm daily Memorial Day-Labor Day).

## Outfitters

The **Adventure Center** (40 N. Main St., 541/488-2819 or 800/444-2819, www.raftingtours.com) offers half-day, full-day, and multiday fishing, rafting, and cycling trips for any size party. The cost of the rafting trips includes gear (wetsuits, splash jackets, etc.), guides, and transport from Ashland. Half-day rafting trips on the Rogue River (9:30am-2pm or 1:30pm-5:45pm, $75) include a snack; the longer white-water picnic trip (8am-4pm, $129) includes lunch. Rated one of the best floats in southern Oregon, the upper Klamath River trip ($135) generally runs 7:30am-5:30pm and includes all meals.

If you like to ride a bike but are not big on pedaling, contact the Adventure Center for information about their Mount Ashland downhill bike cruise. This half-day morning or picnic-lunch ride descends 4,000 feet on 16 miles of quiet paved roads through the countryside to Emigrant Reservoir. The three-hour morning cruise ($65) departs at 8am and includes fruit, pastries, and drinks. The four-hour picnic cruise ($69) departs at 11am and includes a great lunch in a beautiful mountain glade. Bicycles, safety equipment, round-trip transfer from Ashland, and an experienced guide are provided. The Adventure Center also rents mountain bikes by the hour or by the day; the price includes a helmet, a lock, and maps.

## ENTERTAINMENT AND EVENTS

Shakespeare isn't the only act in town. Local companies include the **Oregon Cabaret Theatre** (1st St. and Hargadine St., 541/488-2902, www.oregoncabaret.com), with musical revues in a club setting, and Southern Oregon State College productions.

Ashland's biggest summertime event, aside from the Shakespeare Festival, is the **Fourth of July parade,** which is more of an exuberant and slightly wacky celebration of the community than a patriotic event.

### ◖ Oregon Shakespeare Festival

While Lithia Park is the heart of Ashland, Shakespeare is the soul of this community. The festival began when Angus Bowmer, an English professor at Ashland College, decided to celebrate Independence Day weekend in 1935 with

Catch the free nightly Green Show during the Oregon Shakespeare Festival.

a Shakespeare production. The city fathers were so unsure of the reception it would get that they asked him to allow boxing matches on the stage during the day prior to the performance. By the time he retired as artistic director of the festival in 1971, his Fourth of July dream had grown into an internationally acclaimed drama company with three theaters, one named in his honor.

Performances run from mid-February through late October or early November, though the famed outdoor **Elizabethan Theatre,** built on the site of Ashland's Chautauqua Dome and modeled after the Fortune Theatre of London circa 1600, is open in summer only. This is the largest of the festival's three theaters and primarily the domain of the Bard. While Shakespeare under the stars is incredibly romantic, it can also get very cold after sunset. Curtain times run 8pm-8:30pm with most shows ending around 11pm. This outdoor theater opens in early June and closes by mid-October.

The second-largest playhouse is the 600-seat **Angus Bowmer,** an indoor complex with excellent acoustics, computerized sound and lighting, and nary a bad seat in the house. Finally, the 150-seat **Thomas Theatre** is where modern works and experimental productions are the norm. This theater is small enough to stage plays that might be overwhelmed by a larger venue.

In addition to the plays themselves, two other events are popular with theatergoers. **Backstage Tours** (10am Tues.-Sun., high season $13 adults, $9 youth ages 6-17, reservations required) explore the history, design, and technology of all of the festival's repertory theaters, including the fascinating Elizabethan Stage. The regular tour is a walking tour and has six flights of stairs; call ahead to schedule a tour without stairs.

Catch the free **Green Show** on the plaza outside the Elizabethan Theatre. It begins at 6:45pm and features live music, lectures, performance, storytelling, and other entertainment. It ends just before 8pm when the outdoor performance starts in the Elizabethan Theatre.

### TICKETS

Getting tickets to the **Oregon Shakespeare Festival** (15 S. Pioneer St., Ashland, OR 97520, 541/482-4331 or 800/219-8161, www.osfashland.org, box office 9:30am-performance time Tues.-Sun., 9:30am-5pm Mon., closed most holidays) is as much a part of the show as the performance. Due to tremendous popularity, seats sell out months in advance. All seats are reserved; ticket prices range $25-96. Children under age six are not permitted. Once tickets are purchased, there are no refunds.

If you are unable to get advance tickets, your best bet is to show up at the Shakespeare Plaza an hour or two before the show with a sign stating what show you want to see. If you are lucky, you will score tickets from someone with extras. Avoid bidding wars with other would-be theatergoers, as ticket scalping is frowned upon. Otherwise, be at the ticket window at 6pm; any available seats will be released at that time. And remember, there is no late seating.

## ACCOMMODATIONS

Quoted rates are for June-September; expect prices to drop around one-third outside the summer high season. Ashland's high cost of living is reflected in the rack rates of the town's accommodations. Nonetheless, there's generally something to be found to meet the needs of most every budget. If Ashland's prices seem too high, you can find less expensive rates in Medford, a 10-minute drive to the north.

The warm traditions of Britain are represented in Ashland not only by the Oregon Shakespeare Festival but also by the town's numerous bed-and-breakfasts, the most of any locale in the state. Many B&Bs require a two-night minimum stay during summer. The **Ashland Bed and Breakfast Network** (800/944-0329, www.abbnet.com) can help you find quality B&B lodgings in town.

### Under $50

Offering dorm beds and a handful of private rooms, the **Ashland Hostel** (150 N. Main St., 541/482-9217, www.theashlandhostel.com,

$28 pp dorm bed, $45-59 d private room with shared bath, $79 family room with private bath) is a two-story 1902 house near the Pacific Crest Trail, only three blocks from the Elizabethan Theatre and Lithia Park and two blocks from the Greyhound station. Reservations are essential, especially March-October. The hostel has a coin-op laundry.

A newer hostel, **Ashland Commons** (437 Williamson Way, 541/482-6753, www.ashlandcommons.com, $26 pp dorm bed, $45-65 pp private room), is a little farther from the downtown hub in a quiet residential neighborhood.

## $50-100

Moderately priced guest rooms are available from **Cedarwood Inn** (1801 Siskiyou Blvd., 541/488-2000 or 800/547-4141, www.ashlandcedarwoodinn.com, $82-92), with a pool and continental breakfast. Two-bedroom and kitchen units are also available.

## $100-150

The **Ashland Motel** (1145 Siskiyou Blvd., 541/482-2561 or 800/460-8858, www.ashlandmotel.com, $105-115) offers good value and clean, cheery, and basic pet-friendly guest rooms. All rooms have fridges and microwaves; there are two 2-bedroom units, and a small outdoor pool.

A dollar-wise choice with some charm is the **Columbia Hotel** (262½ E. Main St., 541/482-3726 or 800/718-2530, www.columbiahotel.com, $125-169), in the center of town. This well-kept 1910 hotel with a grand piano in the lobby has 24 rooms. Most rooms share bathrooms. Rooms at a sister property, **◖ The Palm** (1065 Siskiyou Blvd., 877/482-2635, www.palmcottages.com, $103-169), are in a well-maintained cottage-style motel in the midst of lovely gardens. A saline pool, sundeck, and cabanas complete the oasis-like atmosphere. During the off-season, the Palm accepts pets in some rooms.

Out at the interstate exit is the **La Quinta Inn** (434 W. Valley View Rd., 541/482-6932 or 800/527-1133, www.lq.com, $119-144), with

an indoor pool, a business center, and guest laundry.

The **Pelton House** bed-and-breakfast (228 B St., 541/488-7003 or 866/488-7003, www.peltonhouse.com, $135-185) is located in a historic Victorian just a few blocks from the Shakespeare Festival. Each of its seven rooms is has an earthy theme, and two suites are available for families or groups.

## $150-200

If you don't want to spend a bundle on lodging but want to stay in the center of Ashland, **Best Western Bard's Inn Motel** (132 N. Main St., 541/482-0049 or 800/533-9627, www.bardsinn.com, $169-199) is a good choice. Just across the Main Street bridge from downtown, the Bard's Inn is no more than five minutes' walk from the theaters. There are a number of room types, all nicely furnished and well maintained. Facilities include a streamside restaurant and bar.

Clean and meticulously maintained, a privately owned and operated premium motel is the **Stratford Inn** (555 Siskiyou Blvd., 541/488-2151 or 800/547-4741, www.stratfordinnashland.com, $165-185), just five blocks from the theaters with reserved parking for guests. All guest rooms have a fridge, and a couple of kitchen suites are available. Free laundry services, free ski lockers during ski season, an elaborate continental breakfast, and an indoor pool and whirlpool tub all contribute to the inn's high occupancy rate.

The 70-room **Ashland Springs Hotel** (212 E. Main St., 541/488-1700 or 888/795-4545, www.ashlandspringshotel.com, $179-229), on the corner of 1st and Main Streets (a block from the Elizabethan Theatre), is a first-class historic hotel. When it opened in 1925, it was considered a skyscraper; at nine stories it's still the tallest building between San Francisco and Portland. It languished in obscurity for decades until its multimillion-dollar restoration a few years back, but it still evokes the grandeur of the past. A grand ballroom, a bar to enjoy parlor games and musical entertainment in, and English gardens add

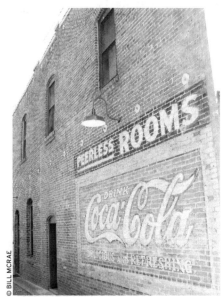

The Peerless Hotel is one of the most elegant hotels in Ashland.

touches evocative of another era. Luxuriously appointed guest rooms aren't large but boast oversize windows highlighting nice views. Minimum stays may apply.

The historic **❨ Peerless Hotel** (243 4th St., 541/488-1082 or 800/460-8758, www.peerless-hotel.com, $165-229) was established in 1900 when the railroad came to Ashland. It served the needs of railroad travelers for many years before falling into disuse. The old hotel was brought back to life in the 1990s, when it was thoroughly modernized and converted into a boutique B&B-style hotel. One of the most distinctive places to stay in Ashland, the Peerless also offers a fine dining restaurant and a location in the art gallery-rich Railroad District.

The **❨ Morical House Garden Inn** (668 N. Main St., 541/482-2254, www.moricalhouse. com, $151-270) is a restored 1880s farmhouse with seven rooms and a guesthouse with three luxury suites, each with a picture-postcard view of Grizzly Mountain and the Siskiyou foothills. Wood floors, stained-glass windows,

and antiques sustain the "good old days" theme despite the many modern conveniences. In season, the two acres of gardens provide organic produce for breakfast as well as a wide variety of herbs and flowers. Many species of birds and butterflies are attracted to the gardens, which are tastefully accented by a waterfall and stream meandering through the grounds. Given all this, it's sometimes hard to remember that you are only a few blocks away from downtown theaters and shopping.

**Plaza Inn and Suites** (98 Central Ave., 541/488-8900 or 888/488-0358, www.plazainn-nashland.com, $179-229) is a large, modern hotel just below downtown and within easy walking distance of the theaters. Many of the rooms look onto a parklike courtyard that fronts onto Ashland Creek. Guest rooms are very nicely appointed; many have balconies and some allow pets. A breakfast buffet is included in the rates.

The **❨ Chanticleer Inn** (120 Gresham St., www.ashland-bed-breakfast.com, 541/482-1919, $185-205) rules the roost with five romantic guest rooms replete with fluffy comforters and private baths. Dogs are permitted (with prior approval) in some of the rooms. The gourmet breakfasts are the talk of Ashland. Round-the-clock refrigerator rights, complimentary wines and sherry, and a full cookie jar on the kitchen counter help keep you wined and dined throughout your stay.

**Anne Hathaway's Cottage** (586 E. Main St., 541/488-1050 or 800/643-4434, www.ash-landbandb.com, $175-195), four blocks from the theaters, boasts fresh-cut flowers, down comforters, firm beds, and private baths. This building was once a boardinghouse; the cottages across the street are now part of this B&B complex.

The **Abigail's Bed and Breakfast Inn** (451 N. Main St., 541/482-4563, www.abigails-bandb.com, $165-175, cottage $250) is an elegantly restored Victorian home with antique furniture and private baths, plus a garden cottage with a fully equipped kitchen, a living room, and two bedrooms, making it well-suited for families and groups of up to six.

© BILL MCRAE

The **Iris Inn** (59 Manzanita St., 541/488-2286 or 800/460-7650, www.irisinnbb.com, $190) is a cheerful Victorian with a fitting decor four blocks from the theaters. Full breakfast in the morning, cold drinks during the day, and wine and sherry at night add to the welcoming atmosphere.

The **McCall House** (153 Oak St., 541/482-9296 or 800/808-9749, www.mccallhouse.com, $190-250) is a restored Italianate mansion built in 1883 by Ashland pioneer John McCall. A National Historic Landmark, this nine-room inn is a block from restaurants, shops, theaters, and Lithia Park. Delectable fresh-baked goodies with juice or tea are served each afternoon. The Carriage House offers two beds and a kitchenette.

Two blocks south of the theaters is the acclaimed **Winchester Country Inn** (35 S. 2nd St., 541/488-1113 or 800/972-4991, www.winchesterinn.com, $195-240), offering 19 guest rooms and suites with private baths and loads of personality. The individual attentiveness of the large staff recalls a traditional English country inn. Bay windows, private balconies, and exquisite English gardens add further distinction. Gourmet delicacies are featured at breakfast, and dinner and Sunday brunch are available in the inn's restaurant. Visit the website to check out their changing special lodging packages.

Bathe in naturally occurring hot springs at the **Lithia Springs Inn** (2165 W. Jackson Rd., 541/482-7128 or 800/482-7128, www.ashlandinn.com, $179-199). A couple of miles from downtown amid four acres of gardens, the inn is close enough to access Ashland culture yet far enough away for some real peace and quiet. Twelve of the 14 rooms have whirlpools fed from the hot springs. There are eight cottage suites, two theme suites, and four regular guest rooms available. Most of the one- and two-room cottages adjacent to the lodge feature a fireplace, a refrigerator, a wet bar, and a double Jacuzzi. Be sure to book well in advance.

Though it's just eight miles from Ashland, you'll feel light-years from the Bard at **Callahan's Mountain Lodge** (7100 Old Highway 99 S., 541/482-1299 or 800/286-0507, www.callahanslodge.com, $165-220), a massive log lodge high in the Siskiyou Mountains on the road to the Mount Ashland ski area (take I-5 Exit 5). There are only 19 rooms in the atmospheric lodge, and they book up fast in ski season. But the lodge is open year-round, and the rooms are comfortably furnished in a rustic Western style. As notable are the stone fireplaces, patios, nightly live music, and friendly bar and restaurant, making this a popular spot for rendezvous and entertainment.

## Over $200

At the **[** **Ashland Creek Inn** (70 Water St., 541/482-3315, www.ashlandcreekinn.com, $265-425) you won't get any closer to Ashland Creek without getting wet. This small luxury-level inn is directly adjacent to the stream and has several guest rooms with cantilevered decks directly above the rushing water. Each of the 10 suites is uniquely decorated according to a theme—the Caribe, the Marrakech, the Edinburgh—and each offers complete kitchens, living rooms, private entrances, and decks. Best of all, this comfort and style are just moments from downtown shopping and the theaters.

## Camping

**Emigrant Lake** (5505 Hwy. 66, 541/774-8183, www.co.jackson.or.us, $20 tent, $30 RV), a few miles east of Ashland, has RV and tent camping at a Jackson County Parks Department campground. South of town, **Mount Ashland** has a primitive campground (free, no water) about a mile past the ski resort.

On the northern edge of town, **Jackson WellSprings** (2253 Hwy. 99 N., 541/482-3776, $20 one person in tent, $28 for two) has tent sites on a grassy, tree-shaded lawn. It's highly informal (with a hippie vibe, to be truthful) and gets a bit of road noise, so it's not for the faint of heart. However, camping does gain you admission to the pool, sauna, and steam room, and it's only about a five-minute drive from downtown.

Emigrant Lake, about five miles east of Ashland, is a good place to camp.

## FOOD

Ashland's creative talents are not just confined to theatrical pursuits; some of Oregon's better restaurants can be found here. Even the humbler fare served in Ashland's unpretentious cafés and pubs can be memorable. The city has a 5 percent restaurant tax, a surcharge seen nowhere else in the Beaver State except Lincoln City.

Stock up on groceries or pick up a deli sandwich at the **Ashland Food Co-op** (237 N. 1st St., 541/482-2237, 7am-9pm daily).

### Bakeries and Cafés

Find Ashland's best coffee and a friendly place to hang out for a while at **Noble Coffee** (281 4th St., 541/488-3288, 7am-4pm daily), in the hip railroad district. Right downtown, **Four and Twenty Blackbirds** (1604 Ashland St., 541/488-0825, 8am-5pm Mon.-Fri., 8am-1pm Sat.) is the place to pick up morning muffins or a fruit pie for later. Another friendly spot for pastries and desserts is **Mix Sweet Shop** (57 N. Main St., 541/488-9885, 7am-9pm daily), with Stumptown coffee and a bohemian atmosphere.

### American

For Ashland's most popular breakfast café, head to **Morning Glory Restaurant** (1149 Siskiyou Blvd., 541/488-8636, 8am-1:30pm daily, $10-12) for delicious omelets, pancakes, and breakfast sandwiches. This place is not a secret, and lines on weekend mornings can be long.

The second-floor patio at the **Greenleaf Restaurant** (49 N. Main St., 541/482-2808, 8am-9pm daily, $10-20) is a great spot to enjoy a meal. The menu offers lots of vegetarian choices, with pasta, stir-fries, salads, and sandwiches in addition to Mediterranean main courses like chicken piccata and red snapper Palermo.

New York meets the Pacific Northwest at **Brothers Restaurant** (95 N. Main St., 541/482-9671, 7am-2pm daily, $3-13), which offers breakfast all day, excellent omelets and bagel sandwiches, plus deli sandwiches for lunch.

**Alex's** (35 N. Main St., 541/482-8818, 3pm-9pm Mon.-Thurs., 3pm-10pm Fri., 11:30am-10pm Sat., 11:30am-9pm Sun., $9-17) serves pasta and other light entrées in a historic second-story bar and dining room flanked by fireplaces.

**Pangea Grills and Wraps** (272 E. Main St., 541/552-1630, 11am-8pm daily, $7-11) is a soup, salad, and wraps emporium featuring free-range meats along with many vegetarian, vegan, and wheat- or gluten-free choices. The preparations are light, flavorful, and reasonably priced. This place is perfect for a quick meal before the show on a hot midsummer night.

## Asian

The **Thai Pepper** (84 Main St., 541/482-8058, 11:30am-2pm Tues.-Sat., 5pm-9:30pm daily, $9-18) has a lot to offer: Not only is the spicy, flavorful Southeast Asian cuisine well prepared and moderately priced, the dining room steps down into the steep gulch of Ashland Creek, offering a cool and quiet haven in the summer heat and one of the most pleasant patio dining areas in town.

**Kobe** (96 N. Main St., 541/488-8058, 5pm-10pm Sun.-Thurs., 5pm-11pm Fri.-Sat., rolls from $7-16) offers top-quality sushi, sashimi, hand rolls, and an assortment of small plates that showcase contemporary Japanese cuisine.

For East Indian food, go to **Taj** (31 Water St., 541/488-5900, 11am-3pm and 5pm-9:30pm daily, $15-22), which has a number of vegetarian dishes, traditional curries, and tandoor oven specialties. At lunchtime, enjoy the $9 buffet.

## Pizza

Stop by **Martoli's** (38 E. Main St., 541/482-1918, 11am-9pm Sun.-Thurs., 11am-10pm Fri.-Sat., $11-22) for a slice or a whole pizza. It's the best pizza in town, and the cafe is a cheery place with a Deadhead theme.

## Latin American

A fun and exciting place to explore new tastes is **Tabu** (76 N. Pioneer St., 541/482-3900, www.

tabuashland.com, 11:30am-9pm daily, tapas till late, $8-21), a restaurant that takes the zesty foods of Central America and updates them with new flavors and preparations. Choose from entrées like banana leaf-wrapped fish or guava chipotle ribs, or select a series of tapas. The cocktail bar at Tabu is a favorite late-night haunt of thespians.

## Pacific Northwest

The restaurant at the historic Winchester Inn has undergone a transformation. Fittingly, it's now the **Alchemy Restaurant** (35 S. 2nd St., 541/488-1115, www.alchemyashland.com, 4pm-9pm Wed.-Sat., 9:30am-12:30pm and 4pm-9pm Sun., dinner $23-35, brunch $9-14) and serves sit-up-and-take notice modern cuisine prepared with rarified techniques and ingredients. In the stately dining room, you can savor sous-vide lamb loin scented with vanilla bean, or bacon-wrapped quail stuffed with chestnuts and minced guinea fowl. The bar is a classy spot to enjoy a cocktail.

The **C Peerless Restaurant** (265 4th St., 541/488-6067, 5:30pm-9pm Tues.-Sat., $24-38) is part of a picturesque historic hotel; the garden is spectacular, so dine al fresco if possible. The impressive selection of small plates ($6-18) makes casual dining fun and exciting—start with chorizo-stuffed dates or lamb meatballs with blue cheese filling, and keep the plates coming. The menu also offers à la carte fine dining (salmon, steaks, pasta), but you'll find it hard to resist the small plates.

**C Amuse** (15 N. 1st St., 541/488-9000, 5:30pm-9pm Tues.-Sun., $22-34) is Ashland's top French-via-Pacific-Northwest restaurant, with a menu that changes weekly and features fresh local fruit, vegetables, and mushrooms as well as ranch beef and lamb and locally harvested fish. Expect such sophisticated dishes as crispy veal sweetbreads with roasted mission figs or black truffle-roasted game hen. Desserts are especially good. The small dining room is deceptive; the back patio is shady and expansive.

Just down the road from Ashland is the

absolutely unique **❰❰ New Sammy's Cowboy Diner** (2210 S. Pacific Hwy., 541/535-2779, noon-1:30pm and 5pm-9pm Wed.-Sun., $18-28, three-course prix fixe $50). The chef-owners are Bay Area expatriates who moved to Ashland with retirement in mind but somehow got talked into cooking for friends, then for the public, a few nights a week. The menu changes frequently, but expect delicious fish, rabbit, pork, and charcuterie, all prepared with great care and skill—if the braised beef ribs are offered, by all means order them. The wine list is very imposing, with hundreds of choices. The dining area has recently expanded, but to understand why New Sammy's has such a devoted following, ask to be seated in the old dining room with cow wallpaper and just six tables in what was once a gas station. Call for winter hours; reservations are strongly recommended.

Head down to Ashland Creek and search a bit to find the door to the **❰❰ Loft** (18 Calle Guanajuato, 541/482-1116, http://loftbrasserie.com, 5pm-9pm Tues.-Sun., $13-28), an upstairs brasserie with a patio overlooking the creek. The French-Oregonian menu features locally sourced food including seared steelhead trout served with tasty brussels sprouts and traditional rabbit paté.

Classy but casual, **Coquina** (542 A St., 541/488-0521, www.coquinarestaurant.com, 5pm-10pm Tues.-Sat., $18-32) serves refined Pacific Northwest cuisine based on local, seasonal ingredients. This Railroad District restaurant features such tempting creations as rabbit ravioli with porcini mushrooms and onion jam, and fresh scallops with pea tendril salad.

## Steak Houses

**Omar's** (1380 Siskiyou Blvd., 541/482-1281, 11:30am-2pm and 5pm-9pm Mon.-Thurs., 11:30am-2pm and 5pm-10pm Fri., 5pm-10pm Sat., 5pm-9pm Sun., $13-33) is Ashland's oldest restaurant (mastodon bones were found when excavating for the restaurant in 1946) and its only traditional steak house. Come for hand-cut steaks, fresh seafood, and a broad selection of eclectic main dishes, such

as chipotle-cranberry roast chicken, all served in a darkly atmospheric dining room. For the quality, the prices are very moderate.

Find nose-to-tail meat-centric cuisine at **Smithfields** (36 S. 2nd St., 541/488-9948, www.smithfieldsashland.com, 11:30am-2:30pm and 5pm-9:30pm Tues.-Fri., 10am-2:30pm and 5pm-9:30pm Sat.-Sun., $15-30). The chef-owner, an expat Brit, named the restaurant after a famous London meat market, but it has a down-to-earth Oregon vibe. Don't miss the charcuterie board, with everything made in-house; the Scotch quail egg appetizer is also good.

## Brewpubs and Wine Bars

One story above Ashland Plaza, the **Black Sheep Pub and Restaurant** (51 N. Main St., 541/482-6414, 11:30am-1am daily, $6-25) is a vast Olde English pub with better-than-average fare plus a wide selection of British and Pacific Northwestern ales. This is the place to come for a late-night after-theater supper (burgers, steak pie, grilled salmon) with frothy pints of beer.

Bright, airy, and with a delightful back patio open in good weather, **❰❰ Standing Stone Brewing Company** (101 Oak St., 541/482-2448, 11:30am-midnight Mon.-Sat., 8am-midnight Sun., $8-19) has one of the most pleasant dining rooms in Ashland. Not only are the beers tasty, the menu is also very broad, including soups, salads, burgers, wood-fired pizzas, and entrées verging on fine dining.

Tucked down near Ashland Creek, the **Caldera Tap House** (31 Water St., 541/482-4677, 4pm-10pm Sun.-Tues., 4pm-11pm Wed.-Thurs., 4pm-midnight Fri.-Sat., $6-22) serves some of the best locally brewed beer (it's not brewed on-site, but at a brewery on Clover Lane) along with fairly typical pub food and live music. Caldera is known for packaging its beer in cans, and the canned IPA is terrific. Of course, at the tap house, the brew flows from taps.

If you're looking for a glass of wine or cocktail plus a delicious selection of snacks, then try **Liquid Assets** (96 N. Main St., 541/482-9463, 3am-midnight daily, small plates $8-20), a wine

## INFORMATION

**Ashland Visitor Information Center** (110 E. Main St., 541/482-3486, www.ashlandchamber.com, 9am-5pm Mon.-Fri.) offers brochures, play schedules, and other up-to-date information on happenings.

The **Oregon Welcome Center** (60 Lowe Rd., 541/488-1805, 9am-10pm daily mid-May-Sept.) offers travel information on the whole state. The center is just off I-5 at Exit 19.

## GETTING THERE AND AROUND

The local airport is in Medford. United Express and Horizon Air fly into **Medford/Jackson County Airport** (1000 Terminal Loop Pkwy., 541/772-8068 or 800/882-7488, www.co.jackson.or.us), 15 miles north of town.

**Amtrak** (800/872-7245) has a station 70 miles east at Klamath Falls and 75 miles south at Dunsmuir, California. **Greyhound** (91 Oak St., 541/482-2516) serves Ashland with a handful of daily northbound and southbound departures.

Local connections between Medford and Ashland are possible through **Rogue Valley Transportation** (541/779-2877, www.rvtd.org). Pick up a bus schedule at area businesses or libraries, or on the website.

© BILL MCRAE

Caldera Tap House is tucked below the street, right on Ashland Creek.

bar with a good choice of cheeses and cured meats, plus tempting house specialties such as Dungeness crab cakes, warm chèvre salad, and roast lamb loin with chimichurri.

# Medford

Along with a resource-based economy revolving around agriculture and timber products, Medford (population 73,500) is becoming established as a retirement center. Some of the enticements are proximity to Ashland's culture, Rogue Valley recreation, Cascade getaways, and rainfall totals that are half those recorded in the Willamette Valley. All that summer heat is good for fruit production—the Rogue River Valley around Medford is a major center for pear production, and wine grapes are displacing dairy cows and berries on area farms.

## SIGHTS
### 🄲 Table Rocks

About 10 miles northeast of Medford are two eye-catching basaltic buttes, **Upper and Lower Table Rocks.** They are composed of sandstone with erosion-resistant lava caps deposited during a massive Cascade eruption about 4-5 million years ago. Over the years, wind and water have undercut the sandstone. Stripped of its underpinnings, the heavy basalt on top of the eroded sandstone is pulled down by gravity, creating the nearly vertical slabs that we see today.

The Table Rocks were the site of a decisive

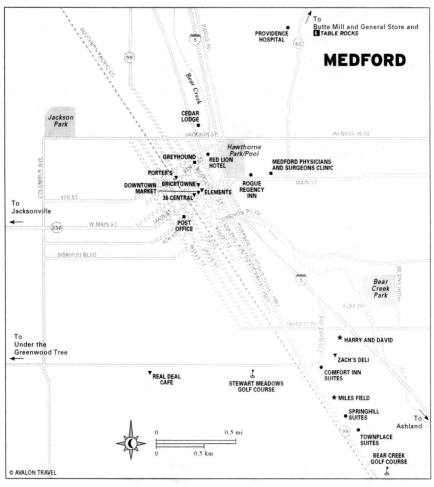

battle in the first of a series of Rogue River Indian Wars in the 1850s. Major Philip Kearny, who later went on to distinguish himself as the great one-armed Civil War general, was successful in routing the Native Americans from this seemingly impervious stronghold. A peace treaty was signed here soon afterward by the Rogue (Takelma) people and the U.S. government. For a time this area was also part of the Table Rock Indian Reservation, but the status of the reservation was terminated shortly thereafter.

The 1,890-acre **Lower Table Rock Preserve** was established in 1979 near the westernmost butte, which towers 800 feet above the surrounding valley floor. The preserve protects an area of special biological, geological, historical, and scenic value. Pacific madrone, white oak, manzanita, and ponderosa pine grow on the flank of the mountain; the crown is covered with grasses and wildflowers. Newcomers to the region will be especially taken by the madrone trees, *Arbutus menziesii*. This glossy-leafed evergreen has a "skin" that peels in warm weather to reveal a smooth, coppery orange bark. It's found mostly in the Pacific Northwest and was noted by early explorers as fuel for long, slow, hot-burning fires.

Park checklists show that more than 140 kinds of plants reside here, including dwarf meadow foam, which grows no place else on earth. One reason is that water doesn't readily percolate through the lava. Small ponds collect on top of the butte, nurturing the wildflowers that flourish in early spring. The wildflower display reaches its zenith in April. A dozen species of flowers cover the rock-strewn flats in bright yellow and vivid purple.

Hikers who take the 2.6-mile trail to the top of horseshoe-shaped Lower Table Rock are in for a treat. Be on the lookout for batches of pale lavender fawn lilies peeking out from underneath the shelter of the scraggly scrub oaks on the way up the mountain. You'll want to walk over to the cliff's edge, which will take you past some of the "Mima mounds" or "patterned ground" that distinguishes the surface of the butte. How the mounds were formed is a matter of scientific debate. Some scientists believe they represent centuries of work by rodents, others think they are accumulated silt deposits, while still others maintain they were created by the action of the wind. However they got there, the mounds are the only soil banks on the mountain that support grasses, which are unable to grow on the lava. Lichens and mosses manage to grow on the lava, however, painting the dull black basalt with luxuriant green and fluorescent yellow during the wetter months.

The **Bureau of Land Management** (3040 Biddle Rd., 541/770-2200, www.blm.gov) has additional information on the Table Rocks.

## HIKING

The trail up Upper Table Rock is a little over one mile but much steeper than the Lower Table Rock trail. Clay clings to the slopes of Upper Table Rock, making the going both sticky and slippery during the wet season. The trail affords wonderful vistas of the Rogue River and Sams Valley to the north.

It reaches the top of the butte on the far eastern side. The ponds up here are smaller and fewer than those on Lower Table Rock, but the Mima mounds are more clearly defined. Upper Table Rock also shows less wear and tear from human activity, and the flower show is just as spectacular. Long black strips of hexagonal basalt look as though they were formed by tanks marching across the butte while the lava was cooling. This irregular knobby surface is difficult to walk on, but the colorful mosses and lichens love it. Also look for the tiny bouquets of grass widows, lovely purple flowers that dangle on long graceful stalks. The odd-looking building off to the west is a navigation device maintained by the Federal Aviation Administration. It's easy to get disoriented out here, with hundreds of acres to explore. The point where the trail heads back down the mountain is marked by two large trees, a ponderosa pine and a Douglas fir, accompanied by a smaller cedar.

To get to the Table Rocks, take Route 62 northeast out of Medford. Take the Central Point exit (Exit 33) east about 1 mile to Table Rock Road and turn north (left). Continue 7.6 miles, passing Tou Velle State Park. Turn east (right) and continue approximately 1 mile to the signed parking lot, which will be on your left. The trail to the top of Upper Table Rock begins here.

## Harry & David

**Harry & David** (1314 Center Dr., 541/776-2277, www.harryanddavid.com), the nation's leading purveyor of mail-order fruit, has a store just off I-5 Exit 27 in the south part of Medford. The fruit-stand section of the large company store offers farm-fresh fruit and vegetables. You can also find rejects from Harry & David's Fruit-of-the-Month Club that are nearly as good as the mail-order fruit but too small or blemished to meet their high quality standards. The jams and fruit spreads are also a bit less expensive than mail order. Perhaps best of all, the store offers a really large selection of Oregon wines, so stop here and ask the friendly staff for recommendations if your trip

© BILL MCRAE

**Harry & David has a long history in Medford.**

spot to stop if you don't have time to explore other wineries because it serves as the tasting room for a number of regional wineries that are too small to maintain their own. There is also a good selection of cheeses and local gourmet items for sale.

**Kriselle Cellars** (12956 Modoc Rd., 541/830-8466, www.krisellecellars.com, 11am-5:30pm daily) is about 12 miles north of Medford, with a stunning new tasting room overlooking the Rogue Valley. The wines here are notable, particularly the French-style viognier and award-winning cabernet sauvignon.

Central Point is home to the **Rogue Creamery** (311 N. Front St., Central Point, 541/665-1155, www.roguecreamery.com, 9am-5pm Mon.-Sat., noon-5pm Fri.), which makes some of the best cheese in the Pacific Northwest, with a focus on blue cheese; the Caveman Blue is exceptionally rich. Stop by Saturday afternoon between 1pm and 3pm for wine tasting.

doesn't allow you to venture into the state's wine country.

Brothers Harry and David Rosenberg took over their family's Bear Creek Orchards in 1914. Bear Creek Orchards was recognized for the size and quality of its pears, which were shipped to the grand hotels of Europe. But the lucrative export market collapsed during the Depression, so the brothers decided to sell their fruit by mail. Harry & David is the oldest mail-order business in the country and, despite recent financial woes, still the nation's largest gourmet fruit and food gift company.

### Wine and Cheese Tasting

**RoxyAnn Winery** (3285 Hillcrest Rd., 541/776-2315, www.roxyann.com) is one of the top wineries in southern Oregon, and conveniently the tasting room is immediately east of Medford in an old pear orchard. RoxyAnn makes particularly good, rich red wines—the claret and syrah are especially delicious. The tasting room is in an old barn, and it's a good

## SPORTS AND RECREATION
### Golf

Near Miles Field is **Bear Creek Golf Course** (2325 S. Pacific Hwy., 541/773-1822). This is a compact nine-hole course that's both a challenge and a bargain at $18 per round on weekdays (on Thursday, it's just $12). **Cedar Links Golf Course** (3144 Cedar Links Dr., 541/773-4373, $16), in northeast Medford, is another beautiful public nine-hole course. To get there, take Route 62 north toward White City and turn right on Delta Waters Road, right again on Springbrook Road, and then left on Cedar Links Drive.

**Eagle Point Golf Course** (100 Eagle Point Dr., Eagle Point, 541/826-8225, www.eagle-pointgolf.com, $45 weekdays, $48 weekends) is arguably the finest course in the Rogue River Valley. Designed by Robert Trent Jones Jr., this 175-acre collection of golf holes boasts enough character to challenge beginners and experts alike. Impressive views of Mount McLoughlin and Table Rocks add to the experience. Carts, clubs, and shoes are available for rent.

Stop at the Rogue Creamery for some of the state's best cheese.

## Swimming

When the summer mercury reaches up into the 90s, it's time to cool off in one of Medford's several public swimming pools. **Jackson Pool** (815 Summit Ave., 541/770-4586, mid-June-early Sept.) is a popular family place. In addition to the 100-foot-long waterslide, a concession stand sells ice cream, soft drinks, and other snacks. A small admission is charged.

## ENTERTAINMENT AND EVENTS

The **Jackson County Fair** (www.jcfairgrounds.com) is held at the county fairgrounds (1 Penninger St., Central Point) just north of town the third weekend in July, with livestock competitions, midway rides, and musical entertainment.

The **Pear Blossom Festival** (www.pearblossomparade.org) takes place the second weekend in April with arts and crafts exhibits, a parade, and a 10K run. The real attraction is the panorama of the pear orchards in bloom

against the backdrop of snowcapped Mount McLoughlin. The parade and run take place downtown, and festivities continue at East Main and Bartlett Streets with more than 100 booths of arts and crafts, food, music, and children's activities.

## ACCOMMODATIONS

Medford has no shortage of motel rooms, with some 30 hotels and motels clustered near the interstate exits. Most are national chains, so there's no mystery as to what you're checking into. The cluster of hotels at I-5 Exit 27 is just 10 miles from Ashland, and all are a good alternative if you can't find affordable rooms there. Medford is the kind of place where it's good to check hotel websites to find deals, since the differences in the hotels aren't great and nearly all are at freeway exits.

### $50-100

You don't have to stay at a freeway exit, however. Just north of downtown on Highway 99 (here known as N. Riverside Ave.) are a number of inexpensive older but well-maintained motels; if you're looking for good value lodgings, come here and check out your options. The closest of these motels to downtown is **Cedar Lodge** (518 N. Riverside Ave., 541/773-7361, www.cedarlodgeinn.com, $55-70), with woodsy lot and a pool. South of town, the quite nice **Pear Tree Motel** (300 Pear Tree Ln., 541/535-4445 or 800/645-7332, www.peartreemotel.com, $75-80) also has a pool.

The closest hotel to downtown is the **Red Lion Hotel** (200 N. Riverside Ave., 541/779-5811 or 800/833-5466, www.redlion.com, $89-119), a full-service establishment that offers room service, laundry and valet service, plus two outdoor pools, a health club, and three dining options.

### $100-150

A number of new upscale hotels have been built in recent years a bit out of town but convenient to I-5. One the nicest is **◖ Rogue Regency Inn** (2300 Biddle Rd., 541/770-1234 or 800/535-5805, www.rogueregency.com, $95-113) which offers an indoor pool and spa, a fitness center, a business center, a complimentary shuttle to the airport, and a bar and restaurant.

Near the airport is **Candlewood Suites** (3548 Heathrow Way, 541/772-2800 or 877/660-8543, $104-128) with large guest rooms, all with kitchenettes.

Another pleasant hotel is **TownePlace Suites** (1395 Center Dr., 541/842-5757 or 800/257-3000, $129-159). On the south side of Medford is **Comfort Inn South** (60 E. Stewart Ave., 541/772-8000 or 866/257-5990, $106-129). **SpringHill Suites** (1389 Center Dr., 541/842-8080, $159-179) has some of the largest guest rooms in Medford.

A romantic bed-and-breakfast with a park-like ambience is ❚ **Under the Greenwood Tree** (3045 Bellinger Ln., 541/776-0000 or 800/766-8099, www.greenwoodtree.com, $140). The guest rooms have private baths and are decorated with antiques, oriental carpets, and beautiful quilts. The house sits on 10 acres of grounds and gardens and features a hammock suspended between enormous 300-year-old oaks, as well as a gazebo beneath shady apple trees overlooking a rose garden.

## FOOD

The local wine industry's recent boom has been the catalyst for a number of excellent new Medford restaurants.

For a locally owned restaurant that offers old-fashioned breakfasts and casual lunches, try the **Real Deal Café** (811 W. Stewart Ave., 541/770-5571, 7am-2pm daily, breakfasts $8-11). Everything is made from scratch at this friendly diner, and in good weather there is seating on a shady patio. Medford's best pizza is at **Kaleidoscope Pizzeria and Pub** (3084 Crater Lake Hwy., 541/779-7787, 11am-9pm Sun.-Thurs., 11am-10pm Fri.-Sat., $10-25), a bit north of town on Route 62. In addition to traditional toppings, Kaleidoscope also features unusual pizza choices like chipotle steak and spicy Thai chicken. There's also a good selection of local microbrews.

**Jasper's Cafe** (2739 N. Pacific Hwy., 541/776-5307, 10:30am-8pm Mon.-Thurs.,

10:30am-9pm Fri.-Sat., 11am-6pm Sun., $5-8) has been a Medford tradition since 1976, and it aims to do just a few things very well. Namely, serve the best hamburgers and hot dogs in the region. The popularity of this small restaurant north of the city often outgrows its seating area, and luckily there are picnic tables to share with other diners. More than 40 different burgers top the menu, all ground fresh daily. The Jasper Dog, loaded with onions, relish, and mustard, is an old-fashioned marvel. Add a hand-scooped milk shake, and you've got an authentic, delicious slice of Americana.

There's a bit of a scene creeping back into long-dormant downtown Medford, where small independent restaurants and bars have found that old storefronts are good spots to offer hand-crafted food and drinks. An excellent spot for lunch is the **Downtown Market Company** (231 E. Main St., 541/973-2233, 11am-4pm Mon.-Fri., noon-4pm Sat., $9-13) which offers fresh flatbreads, panini sandwiches, grilled sausages, and other casual Mediterranean dishes, plus a deli with salads, cheeses, and desserts. You can get your food to go, or take a seat on the patio in the back.

For a traditional steak house atmosphere in Medford, go downtown to the old rail depot, where **Porters** (147 N. Front St., 541/857-1910, 5pm-9pm daily, $13-29) serves pasta, steaks, and plenty of local seafood options, including steelhead trout crusted with hazelnuts and drizzled with blackberry vinaigrette, or slow-cooked prime rib seasoned with rosemary and garlic.

**38 Central** (38 Central Ave., 541/776-0038, 11:30am-10pm Mon.-Fri., 4pm-10pm Sat., $12-27) has a very swank dining room and a cool vibe. The menu offers a number of appetizers that could easily be assembled into a meal—or else, choose from comfort-food selections like "all grown up" mac and cheese or more upscale preparations like halibut and herbed butter steamed in parchment paper.

One of the top places for a relaxed meal with excellent food is ❚ **Elements** (101 E. Main St., 541/779-0135, 4pm-10pm Tues.-Sun., $7-15), a tapas and wine bar. The food is very sophisticated, but the atmosphere is friendly, which makes dishes like serrano-wrapped prawns, cinnamon-cherry seared duck breast, and chorizo-stuffed dates all the more enjoyable.

Downtown also has a couple brewpubs of note. **BricktownE Brewing Company** (44 S. Central Ave., 541/973-2377, www.bricktowne-beer.com, 5pm-10pm Mon.-Tues., 11:30am-10pm Wed.-Sat., noon-6pm Sun., $8-14) offers burgers, sandwiches, salads, and a friendly atmosphere. Housed in a historic fire station, **Portal Brewing Company** (140 N. Front St., 541/499-0848, noon-10pm Wed.-Sun., $6-15) offers good brews plus simple food such as naan pizzas, house-made sausages, and pretzels. For even more fun, head to **Johnny Bs** (120 E. 6th St., 541/773-1900, 11:30am-2am Mon.-Fri., 5pm-2pm Sat., $8-12) for subs, salads, burgers, and chili along with Medford's top selection of live local and touring bands.

The spicy, rich specialties of the American South and the Caribbean are served at **Marco's Pepper Grill** (515 S. Riverside Ave., 541/622-8302, 11am-8pm Tues.-Thurs., 11am-9pm Fri.-Sat., 11am-7pm Sun., $9-17), just south of downtown. The menu spans Tex-Mex favorites, Cajun dishes such as shrimp and sausage jambalaya, and creole street food, all served up with a smile.

**Bambu Asian Café and Wine Bar** (970 N. Phoenix Rd., 541/608-7545, 11:30am-2pm and 5pm-9pm Mon.-Thurs., 11:30am-2pm and 5pm-9:30pm Fri., 5pm-9:30pm Sat., $11-17) features updated and reinterpreted pan-Asian cooking with a mix of small and large plates that encourages sharing and exploring.

## INFORMATION

The **Medford Visitors and Convention Bureau** (1314 Center Dr., 800/469-6307, www.visit-medford.org, 9am-6pm daily) has all kinds of useful maps, directories, and information for the asking. Find their visitors center near the Harry & David store.

## GETTING THERE AND AROUND

A half-dozen buses dock daily at the **Greyhound** station (220 S. Front St., 541/779-2103), running along the I-5 corridor. **Rogue Valley Transportation** (200 S. Front St., 541/779-2877, www.rvtd.org) shares the same station and provides connections to Jacksonville, Phoenix, White City, Talent, and Ashland. Buses run Monday-Friday. **TLC Yellow Cab** (541/772-6288) has 24-hour service in the Medford area.

**Medford/Jackson County Airport** (1000 Terminal Loop Pkwy., 541/772-8068 or 800/882-7488, www.co.jackson.or.us), airport code MFR, is the air hub for southern Oregon and is served by SkyWest, United Express, Horizon, and Allegiant Air.

# Jacksonville

Southern Oregon's pioneer past is vividly preserved in Jacksonville. Five miles west of Medford and cradled in the foothills of the Siskiyou Mountains, this small town of 2,200 residents retains an atmosphere of tranquil isolation. With more than 100 original wooden and brick buildings dating back to the 1850s, it is one of two designated National Historic Landmark Districts in Oregon. (The other is Portland's Old Town.)

Named in honor of President Andrew Jackson and the town's namesake county, Jacksonville was surveyed in September 1851 into 200-foot-square blocks. Then as now, California and Oregon Streets were the hubs of Jacksonville business and social life. But the city's tightly packed wooden structures proved to be especially prone to fire. Between 1873 and 1884, three major fires reduced most of the original buildings to ash. These harsh experiences prompted merchants to use brick in the construction of a second generation of buildings, and the practice was bolstered by an 1878 city ordinance requiring brick construction. Most of the bricks were made and fired locally. To protect them from the elements and the damp season, the porous bricks were painted; cast-iron window shutters and door frames further reinforced the structures.

Boomtown Jacksonville was the first and largest town in the region, and it was selected as the county seat. It was even nominated and briefly considered for the state capital. The prominence of Jacksonville was made manifest with the 1883 erection of a 60-foot-high courthouse with 14-inch-thick walls. But like the gold finds that quickly dwindled, Jacksonville's exuberance faded when the Oregon and California Railroad bypassed the town in the early 1880s in favor of nearby Medford. Businesses were quick to move east to greet the coming of the iron horse, and Jacksonville's stature as a trading center diminished. By the time the county seat was moved to Medford in 1925, Jacksonville's heady days had long since vanished.

During the Depression, families with low incomes took up residence in the town's derelict buildings, taking advantage of the cheap rents. Gold mining enjoyed a brief comeback, with residents digging shafts and tunnels in backyards, but it was not enough to revive the derailed economy. However, the following decades saw a gradual resurgence of interest in Jacksonville's gold-rush heritage. The Southern Oregon Historical Society was created after World War II, and individuals began to care for the many unaltered late-1880s buildings and restore them to their former glory. The Beekman Bank was one of the first structures to be spruced up, and the prominent United States Hotel was rehabilitated in 1964. The restoration movement was rewarded when the National Park Service designated Jacksonville a National Historic Landmark in 1966.

Today, Jacksonville paints a memorable picture of a Western town with its historic buildings, excellent museum, and beautiful pioneer cemetery. In addition, a renowned music festival, colorful pageants, and rich local folklore all pay tribute to Jacksonville's golden age.

## SIGHTS
### Peter Britt Gardens

Peter Britt came to Jacksonville not long after gold was discovered in Rich Gulch in 1851. After trying his hand at prospecting, he redirected his efforts toward painting and photography. The latter became his specialty, and for nearly 50 years he photographed the people, places, and events of southern Oregon (Britt was the first person to photograph Crater Lake). He also incorporated new photographic techniques and equipment in his studio as they developed. You'll find his ambrotypes, daguerreotypes, stereographs, and tintypes on display at the Jacksonville Museum.

The Swiss-born Britt was also an accomplished horticulturalist and among the first vintners in southern Oregon. In addition to experimenting with several varieties of fruit and nut trees to see which grew best in the Rogue River Valley, he kept the first weather data records of the region. Another testimonial to his love of plants is the giant redwood tree on the western edge of the **Britt Gardens** (S. 1st St. and W. Pine St.), which he planted 130 years ago to commemorate the birth of his first child, Emil.

His house was a beautifully detailed Gothic revival home that was built in 1860 and then enlarged in the 1880s. Unfortunately, it was destroyed by fires in 1957 and 1960 and can now be remembered only through photographs. Some of the remaining plantings are part of the original gardens, and many others were lovingly cultivated in 1976 by Robert Lovinger, a landscape architecture professor from the University of Oregon. The Peter Britt Music Festival was held on the grounds of the estate from 1962 until 1978, when the new Britt Pavilion was built just south of Britt's house.

A 0.5-mile hike begins 15 yards uphill from the Emil Britt redwood tree. A fairly level path follows the abandoned irrigation ditch that used to divert water from Jackson Creek to the Britt property. Soon you will notice Jackson

Creek below the trail, as well as several overgrown sections of a nearly forgotten logging railroad bed. This is a particularly nice walk in the spring when the wildflowers are in bloom and the mosses and ferns are green.

## Wine-Tasting

Over 20 wineries are found near Jacksonville, many of them in the Applegate Valley west of town.

Four miles east of Jacksonville is **EdenVale Winery** (2310 Voorhies Rd., 541/512-2955, www.edenvalewines.com, 11am-6pm daily), on the imposing Voorhies estate. EdenVale's most interesting wines are tempranillo, cabernet franc, chardonnay, and red blends. The tasting room also offers sales and samples of wines from other small Rogue Valley vintners.

About eight miles southwest of Jacksonville in the Applegate Valley is **Valley View Winery** (1000 Upper Applegate Rd., 541/899-8468 or 800/781-9463, www.valleyviewwinery.com, 11am-5pm daily). While focused on the grape varieties of southern France, Valley View also makes tempranillo, pinot gris, and port. The Bordeaux-style blends are especially good.

With a tasting room that resembles a French villa, **Troon Vineyard** (1475 Kubli Rd., 541/846-9900, www.troonvineyard.com, 11am-6pm daily) offers zinfandel, cabernet sauvignon, merlot, syrah, and chardonnay, all grown based on organic principles, plus a red blend called Druid Fluid.

The tasting room for **Jacksonville Vineyards** is at **Fiasco Winery** (8035 Hwy. 238, 541/899-9645, www.fiascowinery.com, 11am-5pm daily). You'll taste delicious Bordeaux varietals, plus a light quenching Sangiovese and some interesting red blends.

## ENTERTAINMENT AND EVENTS

The **Peter Britt Music Festival** (Britt Pavilion, 1st St. and Fir St., 541/773-6077 or 800/882-7488, www.brittfest.org) began in 1962 on a grassy hillside amid majestic ponderosa pines

© BILL MCRAE

The Applegate Valley is one of southern Oregon's top wine-growing regions.

near the site of the Britt home. Today, the scope of the small classical festival has broadened into a musical smorgasbord encompassing such diverse styles as jazz, folk, country, bluegrass, rock, and dance, in addition to the original classical repertoire. B. B. King, k. d. lang, the Avett Brothers, the Decemberists, and Ted Nugent are just a few of the artists who have performed here over the years.

The festival runs from the last week of June through the first week of September. Tickets typically range $25-90 for general admission, with most concerts running about $45. Reserved seats are available but are more expensive. Concertgoers often bring along blankets, small lawn chairs (allowed only in designated areas), wine, and a picnic supper to enjoy along with entertainment on balmy summer evenings. Be sure to order your tickets well in advance to avoid having to stand outside. Like the Oregon Shakespeare Festival, some shows sell out months in advance, especially for the well-known performers.

# ACCOMMODATIONS

Most of the lodgings in Jacksonville are bed-and-breakfasts. Several properties in town are run by Country House Inns, which has refurbished Jacksonville's only motel.

## $100-150

The **Wine Country Inn** (830 N. 5th St., 541/899-2050 or 800/367-1942, www.countryhouseinnsjacksonville.com, $129-179) is the only place in town that deviates from the B&B model. Its exterior was designed to resemble historic stage stops along the stage route from Sacramento to Portland.

The **Touvelle House** (455 N. Oregon St., 541/899-3938 or 800/846-3992, www.touvellehouse.com, $139-199) offers five guest rooms and one suite, all with private baths. Each room has its own theme and features touches like antiques, handmade quilts, and tasteful interior decorations. Out back, near the carriage house, is a heated swimming pool. Common areas include a library and a large

living room. A full breakfast is included, and other goodies like fruit and cookies are available for snacking any time.

## $150-200

The **Jacksonville Inn** (175 E. California St., 541/899-1900 or 800/321-9344, www.jacksonvilleinn.com, $159-270, breakfast included) lies in the heart of the commercial historic district. In addition to eight air-conditioned guest rooms in the historic hotel itself, all furnished with restored antiques and private baths, the inn also offers four deluxe cottages complete with antiques, fireplaces, and canopied king beds. The inn has an excellent dining room. Reservations are highly recommended, especially during the summer.

A block down California Street from downtown is the **McCully House Inn** (240 E. California St., 541/899-1942 or 800/367-1942, www.countryhouseinnsjacksonville.com, $169-299). Built in 1861 in the classical revival style, this mansion has four beautifully appointed bedrooms with private baths. European and American antiques, oriental rugs, delicate lace curtains, and a magnificent square grand piano (tuned a half step lower than today's A-440) add to the historical ambience. McCully House also rents guest rooms in other cottages and houses in Jacksonville; see the website for full details.

# FOOD

The **Jacksonville Inn** (175 E. California St., 541/899-1900 or 800/321-9344, www.jacksonvilleinn.com, 7:30am-10:30am and 5pm-9pm Mon., 7:30am-10:30am, 11:30am-2pm, and 5pm-9pm Tues.-Sat., 7:30am-2pm and 5pm-9pm Sun., $19-35) offers steaks, seafood, and specialties of the inn like veal, duck, and prime rib in a Victorian atmosphere of red brick and velvet. Vegetarian dishes are also available. A cellar of over 2,000 wines further enhances your dining experience. There's also a bistro menu after 4pm for lighter appetites, and lovely patio seating during the summer.

The **Bella Union Restaurant and Saloon** (170 W. California St., 541/899-1770, www.

bellau.com, 11:30am-10pm Mon.-Sat., 10am-2pm and 4pm-9pm Sun., $10-23) is another popular spot. Soups, salads, sandwiches, chicken, steaks, pasta, and pizza are some of the items you'll find on the menu. Vegetarians have many choices to select from as well. When the weather is right, the patio behind the restaurant is a pleasant place to eat lunch or enjoy a beer. Also available are picnic baskets, a good choice if you're going to a Britt festival concert. Be sure to call in your order by 2pm.

For the best Thai food in the valley, head for the **Thai House Restaurant** (215 W. California St., 541/899-3585, 11:30am-2pm and 5pm-9pm Mon.-Fri., 5pm-9pm Sat., 5pm-8pm Sun., $12-14).

Ashland's outpost of contemporary fine dining is **C Gogi's Restaurant** (235 W. Main St., 541/899-8699, www.gogis.net, 5pm-9pm Wed.-Sat., 10am-2pm and 5pm-9pm Sun., $23-28), and what an exciting addition it is to Jacksonville's staid dining scene. The dining room manages to be warm and modern at the same time, and the food is absolutely of the here and now. Pan-seared salmon is served with truffle orange-fennel salad, and mushroom-stuffed game hen comes with braised radishes and thyme beurre blanc.

## INFORMATION

The **Jacksonville Chamber of Commerce** (185 N. Oregon St., 541/899-8118, www.jacksonvilleoregon.org, 10am-5pm Mon.-Fri. year-round, 11am-4pm Sat.-Sun. June-Oct., noon-4pm Sat., Nov.-May) has the scoop on events and activities.

## GETTING AROUND

Hop aboard the old-fashioned **Jacksonville Trolley** ($5 adults, $3 children ages 6-12) and learn a bit about local history from a period-dressed guide. Tours depart on the hour (11am-3pm summer) from the historic Beekman Bank at the corner of California and 3rd Streets.

On a hot afternoon, the hills of Jacksonville can seem pretty steep. Join up with **Segway of Jacksonville** (360 N. Oregon St., 541/899-5269, 10am and 2pm Tues.-Sat., $75) and spend a few minutes mastering your steed before heading out on a two-hour guided tour.

Drivers, note that the 25 mph speed limit on the main street through town is strictly enforced.

# Grants Pass

The banner across the main thoroughfare in town proudly proclaims: "It's the Climate." But while the 30-inches-per-year precipitation average and 52°F yearly mean temperature might seem desirable, the true allure of Grants Pass is the mighty Rogue River, which flows through the heart of this community. More than 25 outfitters in Grants Pass and the surrounding villages of Rogue River and Merlin specialize in fishing, float, and jet-boat trips. Numerous riverside lodges, accessible by car, river, or footpath, yield remote relaxation in the shadow of the nearby Klamath-Siskiyou Wilderness.

The city itself is similarly attractive: It has a number of good restaurants, an active downtown area, and a large and dynamic **farmers market** (4th and F Sts., 9am-1pm Sat. mid-Mar.-Thanksgiving). On busy summer days, Grants Pass really buzzes with high spirits and activity.

It's hard to miss the 18-foot-high statue near the north Grants Pass exit (Exit 58) off I-5. Sporting a simulated mammoth skin and a dinosaur-bone club and looking like he just strode in off the set of *The Flintstones*, the **Caveman** has been the official welcome to Grants Pass since 1972. Spawned by a semi-notorious local civic group called the Oregon Cavemen, who also parade around in skins, drink saber-toothed tiger "blood," and eat raw meat during their secret initiation rites, the

Caveman cost $18,000 to build. While many locals have lambasted the city's mascot as portraying a backward redneck image for Grants Pass, it's worth noting that over a dozen businesses and the local high school have proudly embraced the Caveman symbol.

# SIGHTS
## Palmerton Arboretum

Six miles down Route 99 in the town of Rogue River is the **Palmerton Arboretum** (West Evans Creek Rd., Rogue River, 541/776-7001, 8am-dusk, free). Originally a five-acre nursery, the arboretum features plant specimens from around the globe, including Japanese pines and Mediterranean cedars in addition to redwoods and other trees native to the Pacific Northwest. A real treat in the spring, the ornamental arboretum offers over 40 species of mature trees complemented by several kinds of azaleas and rhododendrons. Admission is free. While you're there, be sure to see **Skevington's Crossing,** a 200-foot-high swinging suspension bridge over Evans Creek that connects the arboretum to Anna Classick city park.

## Wildlife Images Rehabilitation and Education Center

Originally a rehabilitation station for injured birds of prey, **Wildlife Images Rehabilitation and Education Center** (11845 Lower River Rd., 541/476-0222, www.wildlifeimages.org, 9am-5pm daily, $12 adults, $7 children ages 4-17) has expanded into an outreach program to aid all kinds of injured or orphaned wildlife as well as to educate the public. Bears, cougars, raccoons, and many other indigenous creatures have been helped by this organization. Once the animals are well enough to survive in the wild, they are released. During the summer, tours are offered hourly on the half hour; in winter, tours are every two hours. Tours last between an hour and an hour and a half; reservations are required for all tours. To get here from 6th Street downtown, head south, turn right onto G Street, continue to Upper River Road, and then onto Lower River Road.

© BILL MCRAE

the Oregon Vortex

## Oregon Vortex

About 10 miles south of Grants Pass on I-5 is the **House of Mystery** at the **Oregon Vortex** (4303 Sardine Creek Rd., Gold Hill, 541/855-1543, www.oregonvortex.com, 9am-4pm daily Mar.-May and Sept.-Oct., 9am-5pm daily June-Aug., $9.75 adults, $8.75 seniors, $7 children ages 6-11). Called the "Forbidden Ground" by the Rogue Native American people because the place spooked their horses, it is actually in a repelling geomagnetic field where objects tend to move away from their center of alignment and lean in funny directions. For example, a ball at the end of a string does not hang straight up and down, and people seem taller when viewed from one side of the room as opposed to the other. Visitors may bring balls, levels, cameras (but not video cameras)—or any other instrument they wish—to test the vortex for themselves. To visit the vortex, you'll need to sign up for a 45-minute tour and demonstration, culminating in a visit to the House of Mystery. It's truly a weird spot, and if nothing else, the drive through stands of madrone trees to the vortex is beautiful.

## SPORTS AND RECREATION
### Rafting

There are many ways to enjoy the Rogue River. Some people prefer the excitement and challenge of maneuvering their own craft down the treacherous rapids. Oar rafts (which a guide rows for you), paddle rafts (which you paddle yourself), and one-person inflatable kayaks are the most widely used boats for this sort of river exploration. The 40-mile section downstream from Grave Creek is open only to nonmotorized vessels, and river traffic is strictly regulated by the National Forest Service. For more information, stop at the **Rand Visitor Center** (14335 Galice Rd., Merlin, 541/479-3735).

Limited float permits (25 issued daily) are needed to float the Wild and Scenic portion of the Rogue, which begins 7 miles west of Grants Pass and runs to 11 miles east of Gold Beach. These permits are prized by rafters around the world—this stretch of the Rogue not only has some of the best white water in the United States, but also guarantees a first-rate wilderness adventure. And yet, it can be a civilized wilderness. Hot showers, comfortable beds, and sumptuous meals at several of the river lodges tucked away in remote quarters of this famous waterway welcome boaters after a day's voyage. Excellent camping facilities are available for those who want to experience nature more directly.

### OUTFITTERS

Many outfitters can be found off I-5 Exit 61 toward Merlin and Galice just north of Grants Pass. Rafters hit Class III and IV rapids a little before Galice and, for 35 miles thereafter, the stiffest white water encountered on the Rogue. **Adventure Center** (541/488-2819 or 800/444-2819, www.raftingtours.com) has half-, full-, and multiday trips on oar or paddle rafts. Their adventures range from the mild to the wild. A half-day trip on the Rogue is $75.

**Galice Resort and Store Raft Trips** (11744 Galice Rd., Merlin, 541/476-3818, www.galice.com) offers full-day raft or inflatable-kayak trips as well as river-craft rentals. A half-day float is $69 and a full day on the river is $99, which includes lunch at the resort.

Another river retreat with attractive packages is **Morrison's Rogue River Lodge** (8500 Galice Rd., Merlin, 541/476-3825 or 800/826-1963, www.rogueriverraft.com), about 16 miles from Grants Pass. Everything from half-day ($75) and one-day ($90) floats and excursions to two-to four-day trips is available; see the website for further details. The longer excursions include either stays at other river lodges or camping along the great green Rogue. Transportation back to Morrison's is included, or your car can be shuttled downriver to meet you at the end of the trip.

**Noah's River Adventures** (53 E. Main St., Ashland, 800/858-2811, www.noahsrafting.com) has been providing quality rafting and fishing trips since 1974. They have half-day ($89) and one- to four-day excursions that vary from exciting white-water rafting highs to

## ROGUE VALLEY MOREL PICKING

Wild mushroom picking can be a fun pastime or a money-making proposition in various parts of Oregon. Morels, a cone-shaped fungus with deeply crenulated caps and short hollow stems, are one of several coveted varieties that fare especially well in the Rogue Valley. The fact that they're easily identifiable, fry up great in omelets, and come out in spring makes them especially popular among residents. Although usually found in forested areas such as the foot-hill below Mount McLoughlin, morels also can be harvested from backyard orchards in Rogue Valley fruit country.

The combination of night temperatures above freezing, high humidity, and daytime temps of 46-60°F is optimum to bring this fungus to fruit. They often pop up in the wake of forest fires or in landscapes disturbed by logging and road building. If it's warm, these mushrooms can be found in late March. When spring conditions hit the lower slopes of the Cascades in the months to follow, pickers usually aren't far behind, in pursuit of what many consider to be the most savory mushroom of all. If you can't find morels in the wild, you should check a local farmers market, where they are generally available from professional mushroom foragers.

kinder, gentler floats. See the website for rates and package details.

**Orange Torpedo Trips** (209 Merlin Rd., Merlin, 541/479-5061 or 866/479-5061, www.orangetorpedo.com) has half-day and one- to three-day adventures on rafts or inflatable kayaks (also affectionately known as "orange torpedoes" because of their color and shape). A six-hour day trip that covers nine miles of the Rogue is $99.

**Ferron's Fun Trips** (210 Merlin Rd., Merlin, 541/479-5061 or 866/479-5061, www.roguefuntrips.com) is a family-run business with guided raft tours and rentals ($25 a day and up). Half-day trips are offered both morning and afternoon ($75) and full-day trips ($95) include lunch. Ferron and his guides bring inflatable kayaks along on all the guided trips for anyone who gets the urge to paddle solo.

**Rogue/Klamath River Adventures** (541/779-3708 or 800/231-0769, www.rogueklamath.com) has one- to three-day white-water rafting and inflatable-kayak trips that give you the option of camping out under the stars or roughing it in style at a river lodge.

For more information on scenic fishing and white-water rafting trips, contact the **Rand Visitor Center** (14335 Galice Rd., Merlin, 541/479-3735) or the **Visitors Information Center** (1995 NW Vine St., Grants Pass, 800/547-5927, www.visitgrantspass.org).

These information outlets can also supply tips on riverside hiking. The Rogue trails out of Grants Pass aren't as remote as their Gold Beach counterparts, and litter can sometimes mar the route. Nonetheless, the fall colors in certain areas along the Rogue along with a profusion of swimming and fishing holes can add a special dimension to your hike.

### Fishing

The upper Rogue River is renowned for one of the world's best late-winter steelhead fisheries. Numerous highways and back roads offer easy access to 155 miles of well-ramped river between Lost Creek Reservoir, east of Medford, and Galice, west of Grants Pass. With fall and spring chinook runs and other forms of river recreation, it's no accident that the Rogue Valley is home to the world's top aluminum and fiberglass drift boat manufacturers. Add rafters, kayakers, and plenty of bank anglers and you can understand why peak salmon or steelhead season is sometimes described as "combat fishing." Contact southern Oregon visitors information outlets for rules, regulations, and leads on outfitters; many of the rafting outfitters listed above also offer guided fishing trips.

## Golf

About 15 minutes north of Grants Pass is **Red Mountain Golf Course** (324 Mountain Green Ln., 541/479-2297, $20 for 9 holes), a small but challenging 2,245-yard executive course.

**Dutcher Creek Golf Course** (4611 Upper River Rd., 541/474-2188, www.dutchercreekgolf.com, $25) is an 18-hole par-70 public course.

## Jet-Boating

You don't have to risk life and limb in a fancy inner tube to see the Rogue: Several local companies offer jet-boat tours. On a jet boat, powerful engines suck in hundreds of gallons of water per minute and shoot it out the back of the boat through a narrow nozzle, generating the necessary thrust for propulsion. With no propeller to hit rocks and other obstacles, these 20-ton machines can carry 40 or more passengers in water only six inches deep. This makes the jet boat an ideal way to enjoy the beauty of the Rogue while keeping your feet dry. Also, many outfitters charter drift boats to visit secret fishing holes for anglers to try their luck landing supper.

**Hellgate Excursions** (953 SE 7th St., 541/479-7204 or 800/648-4874, www.hellgate.com, May 1-late Sept.) is the premier jet-boat operator on this end of the river. Their trips begin at the dock of the **Riverside Inn** (971 SE 6th St.) and proceed downriver through the forested Siskiyou foothills. En route, black-tailed deer, ospreys, and great blue herons are commonly seen. If you're lucky, a bald eagle or a black bear might also be sighted. The scenic highlight is the deep-walled Hellgate Canyon, where you'll look upon what are believed to be the oldest rocks in the state. The least expensive way to experience this adventure is with a "scenic" cruise ticket ($39), but for a bit more money you can step up to a brunch, lunch, or dinner cruise. Another option is the white-water adventure trip that goes beyond Hellgate ($64 adults, lunch available but not included). These excursions feature commentary by your pilot, who knows every eddy in the river. Be sure to call ahead for reservations, as space on all of their runs books up fast.

# ENTERTAINMENT AND EVENTS

The **Josephine County Fair** normally takes place in mid-August at the fairgrounds (1451 Fairgrounds Rd., 541/476-3215) in Grants Pass. In addition to the usual fair attractions such as the carnival, concessions, and 4-H livestock, entertainers perform for enthusiastic crowds. A popular annual competition is the four-wheel tractor pull, in which souped-up farm vehicles attempt to drag a bulldozer (with its blade down) for 100 yards as fast as possible.

# ACCOMMODATIONS

You'll find most motel accommodations clustered around the two Grants Pass exits on I-5,

## ROGUE RIVER ROOSTER CROW

The city of Rogue River, southeast of Grants Pass on I-5, has something to crow about. On the last weekend of June, the **Rogue River Rooster Crow** is held at the Rogue River Elementary School grounds. On Saturday, a parade and street fair (featuring arts, crafts, and food booths) takes over downtown. But the big event occurs early in the afternoon. Farmers from all over Oregon and northern California bring their roosters to strut their stuff and crow to the enthusiastic crowds. Following a fowl tradition established in 1953, the rooster to crow the most times in his allotted time period wins the prize for his proud owner. Then it's the humans' turn, in which well-practiced revelers take their turn in trying mimic a rooster's crow. In the evening there's live music and entertainment in the park, and Sunday brings the Rooster Crow Car Show with legions of antique cars.

though there are a number of good choices right downtown.

## $50-100

Near downtown, find the charming **Buona Sera Inn** (1001 NE 6th St., 541/476-4260 or 877/286-7756, http://buonaserainn.com, $69-95), with wall murals that travel from Grants Pass to Italy. The rooms at this courtyard-style motel are more "grandma's house" than Motel 6, with wood floors and nice linens.

Across the river from downtown is a charming option with riverfront access. **Motel Del Rogue** (2600 Rogue River Hwy., 541/479-2111 or 866/479-2111, www.moteldelrogue.com, $90-145) is a classic 1930s motel that has been lovingly updated but not transformed. Most of the units overlook the river. The motel sits on two acres of parklike property and is very clean, comfortable, and quiet.

There are plenty of midrange hotel chain choices at the I-5 exits, and most of them have pools, allow pets, and include breakfast bars. Two such options are the **Comfort Inn** (1889 NE 6th St., 541/479-8301, $83-95) and the **Best Western Inn at the Rogue** (8959 Rogue River Hwy., 541/582-2200 or 800/238-0700, $100-120).

Just off I-5 about 20 miles north of Grants Pass you'll find the **Wolf Creek Inn** (100 Front St., Wolf Creek, 541/866-2474, www.thewolf-creekinn.com, $95-135), a historic stagecoach hotel.

## $100-150

Also out by I-5, these hotels both have pools and continental breakfast: **Best Western Grants Pass** (111 NE Agness Ave., 541/476-1117, $112-124) and **La Quinta Inn** (243 NE Morgan Ln., 541/472-1808 or 800/531-5900, www.laquinta.com, $109-149).

The **Riverside Inn** (986 SW 6th St., 541/476-6873 or 800/334-4567, www.river-side-inn.com, $129-149) is both right downtown and right on the river. Rooms have decks overlooking the river, and the Hellgate jet-boat excursions depart from just below the hotel. Pets are permitted in some rooms.

Next door, the **◖ Lodge at Riverside** (955 SE 7th St., 541/955-0600 or 877/955-0600, http://thelodgeatriverside.com, $139-199) offers very stylish rooms and suites, many with balconies facing the river. The lobby is in a huge log cabin with a stone fireplace, and in the middle of lush gardens beside the river is an outdoor pool. Just like at the chains, you'll get a free continental breakfast; there's also an evening wine reception.

Many guests use **Morrison's Rogue River Lodge** (8500 Galice Rd., 541/476-3825 or 800/826-1963, www.morrisonslodge.com, $77-210) as a base for raft trips. Morrison's was built in the 1940s as a fishing lodge and now has a small complex of cottages, suites, and lodge rooms, with an outdoor heated pool, basketball court, putting green, bicycles, and wireless Internet.

About 15 minutes north of town and a couple of miles off I-5 Exit 66 is **Flery Manor** (2000 Jumpoff Joe Creek Rd., 541/476-3591, www.flerymanor.com, $140-250). Canopy beds, unique furnishings, and a quiet secluded setting give this country bed-and-breakfast a genteel air. All rooms have nice little touches like plush robes, fresh flowers, and morning coffee and tea service. The breakfast features a health-conscious menu. With a private balcony, a double Jacuzzi, and a fireplace, the Moonlight Suite is the right prescription for a romantic hideaway. Reservations are a must.

## $150-200

One of the premium lodgings in the area is **◖ Weasku Inn** (5560 Rogue River Hwy., 541/471-8000 or 800/493-2758, www.wea-sku.com, $199-329), a venerable river lodge that was the secret retreat of Clark Gable, Walt Disney, Carole Lombard, and other entertainment figures in the 1930s and 1940s. Only 17 guest rooms are available, ranging from lodge rooms and suites to an A-frame cabin. All look out on the Rogue River and have genuine rustic-chic decor. A deluxe continental breakfast is served, as is evening wine and cheese.

The longtime Redwood Motel has undergone a transformation to become **Redwood**

# THE WOLF CREEK INN

Approximately 20 miles north of Grants Pass on I-5 in Wolf Creek is the Pacific Northwest's oldest continuously operated hostelry, the **Wolf Creek Inn** (100 Front St., Wolf Creek, 541/866-2474, www.historicwolfcreekinn. com, $95-135). Originally a hotel for the California and Oregon Stagecoach Line, this historic property, built in 1883, is now owned by the state parks department and is operated as a hotel and restaurant. Legend has it that President Rutherford B. Hayes visited the tavern in the late 1880s, and One-Eyed Charlie used to chew the fat in the dining room. You can also view the small room where author Jack London stayed and wrote part of his novel *The End of the Story*.

Wolf Creek's boardinghouse may have had its heyday in the stagecoach era, but it continues to serve road-weary travelers. The period furniture imparts atmosphere, while the beds and private baths are modern and comfortable; breakfast is included in the room rates. There are no TVs or phones in the rooms, however, in keeping with historic authenticity.

The restaurant (8am-10am, 11am-4pm and 5pm-8pm summer, call for winter hours) serves admirable Pacific Northwest cuisine, with veggies from the inn's gardens and home-smoked meats.

© BILL MCRAE

**Hyperion Suites** (815 NE 6th St., 541/476-0878 or 888/535-8824, www.redwoodmotel.com, $85-225). The venerable motel rooms have been updated and upgraded, and a new structure, with luxury-level suites, has been added. The parklike setting, complete with a grove of redwoods and a 350-year-old Palmer oak, is another plus. Add in a pool, a hot tub, a fitness center, and complimentary breakfast and you've got one of the city's unique lodging options.

## Cabins

About 20 minutes outside of Grants Pass and well within the Wild and Scenic section of the Rogue River is the **Doubletree Ranch** (6000 Abegg Rd., Merlin, 541/476-0120, http://doubletree-ranch.com, Apr.-Oct., cabins $115-145). Originally homesteaded 100 years ago, this 160-acre four-generation working ranch offers cozy cabins, all set up for housekeeping with full kitchens. There's also a five-bedroom house available that is perfect for family groups.

No roads lead to the main lodge and sixteen cabins at **Black Bar Lodge** (541/479-6507, www.blackbarlodge.net, $125 per person includes two meals), but it's a good stop for rafters or hikers along the 40-mile Rogue River Trail. The lodge is built on the site of an old mining claim—the story goes that after the original miner, Mr. Black, was murdered, his body was put into his boat and pushed off down the river. The Black Bar is 10 miles downriver from Grave Creek, and is pretty much off the grid. Generators power lights and electricity, and are turned off at night.

## Camping

The privately owned and operated RV campgrounds tend to be more expensive than their public counterparts but offer more amenities like swimming pools, laundries, showers, and other conveniences. **RiverPark RV Resort** (2956 Rogue River Hwy., 541/479-0046 or 800/677-8857, www.riverparkrvresort.com, $33-44) boasts a tennis/basketball court, hot showers, laundry facilities, and 700 feet of Rogue River frontage to enjoy.

Many fine campgrounds are found along the banks of the Rogue River near Grants Pass, but the only state park in the area is the **Valley of the Rogue** (3792 N. River Rd., Gold Hill, 541/582-1118 or 800/452-5687, www.oregonstateparks.org). About halfway between Medford and Grants Pass off I-5, the park is set along the banks of its namesake river. The Rogue supports year-round salmon and spring steelhead runs. There are 98 sites for trailers and motor homes ($24), 21 tent sites ($19), and a few yurts ($36). This place fills up fast, so reservations are recommended during the warmer months. Hookups, utilities, showers, laundry, and some wheelchair-accessible facilities round out the amenities.

**Indian Mary Park** is the showcase of Josephine County parks. To get here, go about eight miles east of Merlin on the Merlin-Galice Road. Located on the banks of the Rogue River, this campground has 89 sites, several with sewer hookups and utilities, as well as showers, flush toilets, and piped water. A boat ramp, beautiful hiking trails, a playground, and one of the best beaches on the Rogue make this one of the most popular county campgrounds on the river.

**Griffen Park** is a smaller campground with 20 sites for tents and trailers. To get here, take the Redwood Highway (U.S. 199) to Riverbanks Road, then turn onto Griffen Road and follow it about 5 miles to where it meets the Rogue. The park has a boat ramp, showers, flush toilets, piped water, and RV dumping facilities.

**Schroeder Park** is another full-service campground near town. Located on Schroeder Lane off Redwood Avenue, the park has 31 sites, some with hookups and utilities. Showers, flush toilets, and a boat ramp make this a favorite spot for fishing enthusiasts. In addition to a picnic area and an excellent swimming hole, there's a dog park here.

**Whitehorse Park**, 6 miles west of Grants Pass on Upper River Road, has 44 campsites, many with hookups and utilities. Showers, piped water, lighting, and good hiking trails are also found here. The river channel shifted away from the park in the wake of the Christmas flood of 1964, but it's only about 0.5-mile walk to a fine beach on the Rogue.

Sites at Indian Mary, Griffen, Schroeder, and Whitehorse cost $19 for tent sites and $22 for hookup sites. For reservations, call 800/452-5687 or visit www.reserveamerica.com. For more information, contact the **Josephine County Parks Department** (541/474-5285, www.co.josephine.or.us).

# FOOD

Grants Pass has a number of good dining choices, particularly along downtown's G Street. On a summer evening, take a stroll around the neighborhood on this bustling avenue and check out all the options. It's also a good morning destination for fresh roasted organic coffee at **Rogue Coffee Roasters** (237 SW G St., 541/476-6134, 7am-pm Mon.-Fri., 8am-2 Sat.) and pastries from **Dancin Bakery** (1300 SW G St., 541/244-2225).

**Sunshine Natural Foods** (128 SW H St., 541/474-5044, 9am-6pm Mon.-Fri., 9:30am-5pm Sat.) has a café, a salad bar, a juice bar, and an organic food market plus a full line of food supplements and vitamins.

## American

Aficionados of the old-time soda fountain will appreciate the **Grants Pass Pharmacy** (414 SW 6th St., 541/476-4262, 9am-7pm Mon.-Fri., 9am-6pm Sat., $7). Decent sandwiches, sodas, and milk shakes are featured. Local old-timers meet here every afternoon, and it's the kids' first stop after school.

The **Laughing Clam** (121 SW G St., 541/479-1110, 11am-9pm Mon.-Thurs., 11am-10pm Fri.-Sat., $7-27) is an old bar and grill that has been transformed into a lively family-friendly tavern with good sandwiches, pasta, and steaks. The name might suggest that this is a seafood house, which it's not, though a few fish dishes are offered.

Another old-time bar made young again, the **Ⓒ Circle J** (241 SW G St., 541/479-8080, 11am-9pm Mon.-Thurs., 11am-10pm Fri.-Sat., $8-12) is a redbrick cubbyhole with eclectic and

funky decor and a hip and lively clientele. The specialties are pizza, burgers, and sandwiches (including some vegan ones) with sweet potato fries, all washed down with microbrews.

With marvelous views, **Taprock Northwest Grill** (971 SE 6th St., 541/955-5998, 8am-10pm Sun.-Thurs., 8am-11pm Fri.-Sat., $9-26) occupies a very handsome log-built dining room with spacious decks overlooking the river from between the downtown bridges. The menu is geared toward steaks and comfort food, with much of the food grown and produced in the Pacific Northwest; a good selection of sandwiches and salads is also available.

As its name suggests, **The Bohemian** (233 SW G St., 541/471-7158, www.bohemian-bargp.com, 11:30am-11pm Mon.-Fri., 3pm-11pm Sat., $8-17) is a hip bistro and bar with a selection of small and "not so small" plates. You'll find a selection of salads and sandwiches, plus pasta and delectable braised beef with herbed mashed potatoes. There's frequently live music in the evenings.

## International

A somewhat swanky G Street dining room is **Ⓒ Blondie's Bistro** (226 SW G St., 541/479-0420, 11am-9pm daily, $10-21). The international menu includes touches of Indian food such as masala-spiced rack of lamb and Italian food such as chicken marsala or Tuscan grilled shrimp with white beans and wilted greens. A surprising number of vegan options are available.

## Brewpubs and Wine Bars

**Wild River Brewing and Pizza Company** (595 NE F St., 541/471-7487, www.wildriverbrewing.com, 10am-10pm Sun.-Thurs., 10am-11pm Fri.-Sat., $8-16) is a regional standby, with good wood-fired pizza ($16-24 for a large pie), pastas, burgers, and sandwiches and locations in several southern Oregon towns (Grants Pass, Cave Junction, and Brookings Harbor).

A wine bar bordering on a full restaurant, **Ⓒ The Twisted Cork** (210 SW 6th St., 541/295-3094, www.thetwistedcorkgrantspass.

# BED-AND-BREAKFAST IN THE TREES

Located in Takilma near Cave Junction, **Out 'n About Treehouse Institute and Treesort** (300 Page Creek Rd., Cave Junction 97523, 541/598-2208 or 800/200-5484, www.tree-houses.com) is a unique lodging option that's worth driving a bit out of your way to discover. After all, how many bed-and-breakfasts do you find in tree houses?

This comfortable rural retreat blends the whimsy of the 1960s with 21st-century creature comforts. The 10 well-appointed tree-house guest rooms are bolted to 100-year-old white oaks, some 18 feet above the ground. Should you have misgivings about the structural integrity of these accommodations, be advised that the innkeeper gathered nearly 11,000 pounds of his friends to stand on the several units simultaneously—35 times the weight requirements of the local code. Those desiring a more down-to-earth lodging option can stay in a peeled-fir cabin with a cozy woodstove. For the deluxe treatment, reserve a 300-square-foot structure built of redwood and Douglas fir that features a sink, a tub, a fridge, a queen-size futon, a loft, and a 200-square-foot deck with mountain views. The "treepee," a tepee done up in Out 'n About style, is always popular with the kids.

Horseback trail rides, trips to the best Illinois River swimming holes, zip line adventures, and white-water rafting trips can be arranged through the management. Or swim in the river that runs through the property. Rates are $120-160 double (some of the larger tree houses sleep four or more) and up with a two- or three-night minimum stay (Memorial Day-Labor Day) and include continental breakfast. Your stay here will help you better understand tree houses, treeology, and treeminology, and like many other guests, you may well leave a "treemusketeer."

---

com, 11am-3pm Mon., 11am-8pm Tues.-Thurs., 11am-9pm Fri.-Sat., small plates $4-12, main courses $15-20) makes the most of local wines and ingredients. In addition to some 30-odd small plates, flatbreads, salads and soups, the Twisted Cork also offers pasta and house specialty main courses such as blackberry-ancho chile grilled pork and pomegranate cinnamon flank steak. This is one of southern Oregon's most exciting young restaurants.

## INFORMATION

The **Grants Pass/Josephine County Visitor Information Center/Chamber of Commerce** (1995 NW Vine St., 541/476-7717, www.visitgrantspass.com) is open 8am-5pm daily in summer, 8am-5pm Monday-Friday in winter.

## GETTING THERE

**Greyhound** (460 NE Agness Ave., 541/476-4513) offers access to the I-5 corridor.

## CAVE JUNCTION

Sample some of the local wines at **Foris Vineyards** (654 Kendall Rd., 541/592-3752 or 800/843-6747, www.foriswine.com) and **Bridgeview Vineyards and Winery** (4210 Holland Loop Rd., 541/592-4688 or 877/273-4843, www.bridgeviewwine.com). Both wineries offer tastings 11am-5pm daily year-round, although confirm their operating hours in winter.

## ◖ OREGON CAVES NATIONAL MONUMENT

About 30 miles southwest of Grants Pass is the **Oregon Caves National Monument** (Rte. 46, 541/592-3400, www.nps.gov/orca, $8.50 adults, $6 children ages 6-11). The cave itself—as there is really only one, which opens onto successive caverns—was formed over the eons by the action of water. As rain and snowmelt seeped through cracks and fissures in the rock above the cave and percolated down into the underlying limestone, huge sections of the limestone became saturated and

Oregon Caves National Monument

collapsed—much as a sand castle too close to the sea always caves in. When the water table eventually fell, these pockets were drained, and the process of cave decoration began.

First, the limestone was dissolved by the water and carried in solution into the cave. When the water evaporated, it left behind a microscopic layer of calcite. This process was repeated countless times, gradually creating the beautiful formations visible today. When the minerals are deposited on the ceiling, a stalactite begins to form. Limestone-laden water that evaporates on the floor might leave behind a stalagmite. When a stalactite and a stalagmite meet, they become a column. Other cave sculptures you'll see include helicites, hell-bent formations that twist and turn in crazy directions; draperies, looking just like their household namesakes but cast in stone instead of cloth; and soda straws, stalactites that are hollow in the center like a straw, carrying mineral-rich drops of moisture to their tips.

Discovered in 1874, the Oregon Caves attract thousands of visitors annually. During the Depression, walkways and turnoffs were built to make the cave more accessible. Unfortunately, tons of waste rock and rubble were stashed in nooks and crannies in the cave instead of being transported out. This had the effect of obscuring the very formations meant for display. However, the National Park Service started to remove the artificial debris in 1985, exposing the natural formations once again.

The River Styx, another victim of Depression-era meddling, is enjoying a similar resurrection. This stream used to run through the cave but was diverted into pipes to aid trail and tunnel construction. The pipes ended up buried beneath tons of pulverized rock, and now the Park Service is hard at work undoing the work of humans to let the stream flow where nature intended.

## Tours

Tours of the cave are conducted year-round by National Park Service interpreters. Their presentations are both informative and entertaining, and you will leave the cave with a better understanding of its natural, geological, and human history. A recent discovery in an unexplored part of the caverns was a grizzly bear fossil believed to be over 40,000 years old. Children younger than age six must pass ability requirements (e.g., walking up many stairs for a total vertical climb of 218 feet) and stand a minimum of 42 inches tall to gain entry. The tour, limited to 16 people, takes a little over an hour and requires some uphill walking. Good walking shoes and warm clothing are recommended. It may be warm and toasty outside, but the cave maintains a fairly consistent year-round temperature of 41°F. Passageways can be narrow, ceilings low, and the footing slippery. During summer you can wait in line up to an hour to go on a tour, and fewer tours are offered October-April. Call ahead for tour times.

## Accommodations

The six-story **Chateau at Oregon Caves** (541/592-3400, www.oregoncaveschateau.com, May-Oct., $109-170) offers food and accommodations at the caves. About 20 miles east of Cave Junction on OR 46, the château stands at an elevation of 4,000 feet. Built in 1934, this rustic structure blends in with the forest and moss-covered marble ledges. Indigenous wood and stone permeate the building so that you never lose a sense of where you are. The guest rooms feature views of Cave Creek canyon, waterfalls, or the Oregon Caves entrance. For a unique experience, we recommend the sixth floor. The rooms may be small, but they have more character and extend out at odd angles from the building. The Pendleton blankets, tall painted chairs, and wooden bed frames add to the historical nuance.

The château has been nicknamed the "Marble Halls of Oregon," and you can see the huge marble fireplace in the fourth-floor lobby for yourself while you thaw out after your spelunking expedition. The food at the château is high quality, and having Cave Creek running through the center of the dining room definitely adds to the unique atmosphere. Downstairs, the old-fashioned 1930s-style soda fountain (daily May-Oct. 15) dishes up classic American burgers, fries, and shakes.

For a nice after-dinner hike, take the Big Tree Trail, named for a huge Douglas fir estimated to be more than 1,000 years old. With a circumference of 38 feet 7 inches, it is among the largest standing trees in Oregon. The three-mile round-trip wends its way through virgin forest that has tan oak, canyon live oak, Pacific madrone, chinquapin, and manzanita, as well as Douglas fir and ponderosa pine. The hike is not that difficult, and the solitude and views of the surrounding mountains are as inspiring as the Big Tree. For a jaunt that is just under one mile, try the Cliff Nature Trail. Placards will help you identify the plantlife as you traverse the mossy cliffs, and there are also some good vistas of the Siskiyou Mountains.

## Camping

Camping is available at **Grayback** (Wild Rivers Ranger District, 541/592-4000, www.fs.fed.us, $10, water available), a woodsy Forest Service campground 12 miles from Cave Junction on Route 46. There are 39 sites close to Sucker Creek, with one RV hookup and a one-mile hiking trail. Closer to the caves is a smaller Forest Service campground, **Cave Creek** ($10, water); take Route 46 four miles south of the caves to Forest Service Road 4032.

## Getting There

To get to Oregon Caves National Monument, take U.S. 199 to Cave Junction, then wind your way 20 miles up Route 46 (a beautiful old-growth Douglas fir forest lining the road might help distract the faint of heart from the nail-biting turns). The last 13 miles of this trip are especially exciting. Remember that there are few turnouts of sufficient size to enable a large vehicle to reverse direction.

# Roseburg

Many people passing through the Roseburg area (pop. 21,000) might quickly dismiss it as a rural backwater. A closer look, however, reveals many layers beneath the mill town veneer. The number of folks who rely on the woods as a workplace is declining, and although the town still has a no-nonsense sensibility, growing pockets of refinement are now found in between the pickup trucks and lumber mills. An award-winning museum, Oregon's only drive-through zoo, and wineries setting down roots nearby are a few examples.

The true allure of Roseburg is not really in town but in the surrounding countryside. The beautiful North Umpqua River to the east offers rafting, camping, hiking, and fishing. In addition to catching trout, salmon, and bass, anglers come from all over to enjoy one of the world's last rivers with a native run of summer steelhead. Numerous waterfalls along the river and the frothy white water make the Native American word Umpqua ("thundering water") an appropriate name.

## SIGHTS

### Douglas County Museum of History and Natural History

The nationally acclaimed **Douglas County Museum of History and Natural History** (123 Museum Dr., 541/957-7007, www.co.douglas. or.us/museum, 10am-5pm Tues.-Sat., $5 adults, $4 seniors, children ages 17 and under free) is located at the Douglas County Fairgrounds (Exit 123 off I-5). Its four wings feature exhibits that range from a one-million-year-old saber-toothed tiger to 19th-century steam-logging equipment. The museum houses the state's largest natural history collection, and the second-largest collection of historic photos.

### Lotus Knight Memorial Gardens

The **Lotus Knight Memorial Gardens** (5am-10pm daily, free) are in Riverside Park, between Oak Street and Washington Street on the banks of the South Umpqua River. They are alight with colorful azaleas and rhododendrons in the spring.

### Winchester Fish Ladder

The **Winchester Fish Ladder** is just off I-5 at Exit 129 on the north bank of the North Umpqua River. Visitors can watch salmon and steelhead in their native environment as they swim by the viewing window at Winchester Dam. Spring chinook and summer steelhead migrate upriver May-August, and coho, fall chinook, and more summer steelhead swim past September-November. Winter steelhead is the primary species seen going through the fish ladders and on past the window December-May. The Umpqua River offers the largest variety of game fish in Oregon.

### 🄲 Wildlife Safari

Tucked away in a 600-acre wooded valley is Oregon's drive-through zoo, **Wildlife Safari** (Safari Rd., Winston, 541/679-6761 or 800/355-4848, www.wildlifesafari.net, 9am-5pm daily, $18 adults, $15 seniors, and $12 children ages 4-12, no pets allowed).

Once you are inside the park gates, the brightly colored birds and exotic game animals transport you to other lands, with an oddly appropriate Oregon backdrop. Be that as it may, at Wildlife Safari every possible step has been

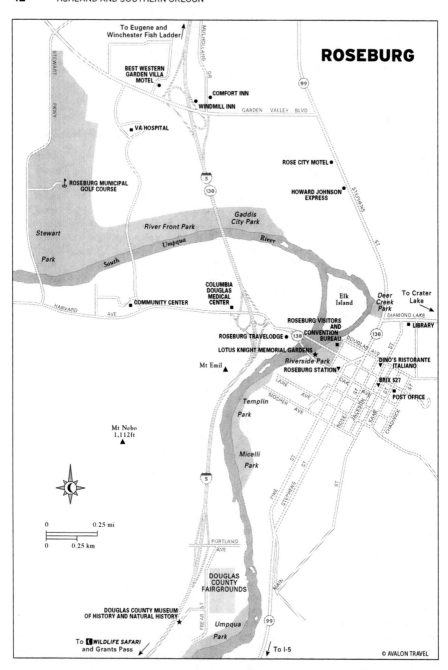

# ROSEBURG

To Eugene and
Winchester Fish Ladder

MULHOLLAND DR

99

STEWART PKWY

BEST WESTERN
GARDEN VILLA
MOTEL

COMFORT INN
WINDMILL INN

GARDEN VALLEY BLVD

VA HOSPITAL

ROSE CITY MOTEL

5

138

HOWARD JOHNSON
EXPRESS

STEPHENS ST

ROSEBURG MUNICIPAL
GOLF COURSE

Gaddis
City Park

Stewart

River Front Park

Umpqua

River

Park

South

COLUMBIA
DOUGLAS
MEDICAL
CENTER

Elk
Island

Deer
Creek
Park

To Crater
Lake

HARVARD    AVE

COMMUNITY CENTER

ROSEBURG VISITORS
AND
CONVENTION
BUREAU

DIAMOND LAKE

138

LIBRARY

ROSEBURG TRAVELODGE

138

DOUGLAS AVE

LOTUS KNIGHT MEMORIAL GARDENS

Mt Emil ▲

Riverside Park

ROSEBURG STATION

DINO'S RISTORANTE
ITALIANO

BRIX 527

OAK ST

POST OFFICE

LANE    AVE

MOSHER    AVE

Templin
Park

ROSE ST

JACKSON ST

KANE ST

CHADWICK

Mt Nebo
1,112ft
▲

Micelli
Park

PINE ST

STEPHENS ST

MAIN ST

5

PORTLAND
AVE

0        0.25 mi

0        0.25 km

DOUGLAS
COUNTY
FAIRGROUNDS

FREAR ST

DOUGLAS COUNTY MUSEUM
OF HISTORY AND NATURAL HISTORY

Umpqua
Park

99

To ◖ WILDLIFE SAFARI
and Grants Pass

To I-5

© AVALON TRAVEL

© WILDLIFE SAFARI

The Wildlife Safari has one of the most successful cheetah breeding programs in the country.

taken to re-create African and North American animal life zones, but with natural prey kept apart from natural predators. Similar precautions are taken with humans and their animal companions. People must remain inside their vehicles except in designated areas, and windows and sunroofs must be kept closed in the big cat and bear areas. Pets must be left in kennels at the entrance ($5 fee for padlock rental).

The first loop takes you to see the tigers and cheetahs. These giant felines loll lazily about or catch catnaps in the tall grass. The next link takes you through the heart of "Africa," where wildebeests, zebras, and other creatures scamper about freely, seemingly oblivious to the slow parade of cars. Elephants, rhinoceroses, and other African big game also make their homes here. Soon you are in "North America." Bears, bighorn sheep, pronghorn, moose, and buffalo are just a few of the animals that live down in the valley.

Throughout the day, many talks and opportunities to watch the animals being fed are scheduled; some are included in the price of admission and some cost extra. Perhaps the most popular attraction is the petting zoo (no extra fee). When the weather is good, you can take a memorable ride on a camel ($7.50) or arrange to help feed the big cats or bears ($95).

With 600 animals, including one of the most successful cheetah breeding programs in the country, Wildlife Safari is involved with various conservation and endangered species programs. After your "safari," pull into the White Rhino restaurant, serving good food within view of lions, giraffes, and white rhinos.

To reach Wildlife Safari, take Exit 119 off I-5 and follow Route 42 for 4 miles. Turn right on Lookingglass Road and right again on Safari Road.

## Wine-Tasting

Several wineries in the Roseburg vicinity offer tasting rooms and tours. The dry Mediterranean climate and rich variety of soils in the area are ideal for chardonnay, pinot noir, Gewürztraminer, Riesling, zinfandel, and cabernet sauvignon varietals. A wine tour pamphlet with a map showing the location of the wineries is available from the **Roseburg Visitors and Convention Bureau** (410 SE Spruce St., 541/672-9731 or 800/444-9584, www.visitroseburg.com), or go to the website www.umpquavalleywineries.org.

**Abacela Vineyards and Winery** (12500 Lookingglass Rd., 541/679-6642, www.abacela.com, 11am-6pm daily) is noted for the large variety of wine grapes grown, including tempranillo, malbec, and dolcetto.

**Girardet Wine Cellars** (895 Reston Rd., 541/679-7252, www.girardetwine.com, 11am-5pm daily) is one of the oldest in the area. Philippe Girardet, from a town at the headwaters of the Rhine River in Switzerland, brings European wine-blending techniques to Oregon. These processes produce unique chardonnay, pinot noir, cabernet sauvignon, and Riesling wines.

The **Henry Estate Winery** (687 Hubbard Creek Rd., Umpqua, 541/459-5120 or 800/782-2686, www.henryestate.com, 11am-5pm daily) has produced a string of award-winning bottlings from chardonnay, Gewürztraminer, and pinot noir grapes. Lunch at shaded picnic tables near the vineyard and the Umpqua River can heighten your enjoyment of the fruit of the vine.

Oregon's oldest vineyard, dating to 1961, is **HillCrest** (240 Vineyard Ln., 541/673-3709, www.hillcrestvineyard.com, 9am-5pm daily Mar.-Dec.). A bewildering range of wine grapes are grown here, but some of the best to sample are the Riesling, syrah, and zinfandel.

## SPORTS AND RECREATION
### Fishing
The Umpqua River system is home to a dozen species of popular sport fish that range from the big chinook salmon to the tiny silver smelt. Visit the **Oregon Department of Fish and Wildlife website** (www.dfw.state.or.us) for additional information on the Umpqua.

Spring chinook enter the North Umpqua River March-June, work their way upstream during July and August, and spawn September-October. Fall chinook are mainly found in the warmer South Umpqua River. Their migration starts in midsummer and peaks in September when the rains increase water flow and lower the river's temperature. The best fishing for summer steelhead on the North Umpqua is June-October; the fish spawn January-March. This fish averages only 6-8 pounds, but it will make you think you are trying to reel in a chinook by the way it struggles.

Coho salmon, alias "silvers," are found throughout the Umpqua River system. The coho life cycle lasts about three years. Each spends its first year in freshwater, heads for the ocean to spend 1-2 years, and then returns to freshwater to spawn. The adults weigh an average of seven pounds each. This fishery has had some lean years recently.

You'll find rainbow trout in nearly all rivers and streams of the Umpqua River system, where the water is relatively cool and gravel bars are clean. This is the river's most common game fish, mainly because the rivers, lakes, and streams of the Umpqua are routinely seeded with over 100,000 legal-size (eight inches or longer) rainbows. The fishing season opens in April, with the best fishing in early summer when the fish are actively feeding.

### Golf
The nine-hole municipal **Stewart Park Golf Course** (1005 Stewart Park Dr., 541/672-4592) charges $16 for 9 holes, $26 for 18 holes; add a few extra dollars on weekends. In addition to power carts, a lighted driving range, and rental golf clubs, a complete pro shop offers lessons and any peripherals you may need.

## ENTERTAINMENT AND EVENTS
Roseburg's big event is the **Douglas County Fair,** held annually at the fairgrounds (Exit 123 off I-5) the second week of August, with down-home events like 4-H livestock competitions, midway rides, food booths, and horse and stock car races. Contact the **Roseburg Visitors and Convention Bureau** (410 SE Spruce St., 541/672-9731 or 800/444-9584, www.visitroseburg.com) for specifics.

If you happen to be in Roseburg on a

© BILL MCRAE

McMenamins Roseburg Station pub is in the old railway depot.

summer Tuesday evening, check out **Music on the Halfshell** (www.halfshell.org), a series of outdoor summer concerts held at the band shell in **Stewart Park** (NW Stewart Pkwy. and NW Harvey Ave.). The free concerts have featured big-name national and international stars such as David Grisman, Taj Mahal, and Pink Martini. The park's bandstand is near the banks of the South Umpqua River.

## ACCOMMODATIONS

There are over 1,500 motel rooms in Roseburg, and the competition keeps rates relatively low.

Budget travelers can bunk down at the **Roseburg Travelodge** (315 W. Harvard Ave., 541/672-4836, $60-70). It's right on the Umpqua, though you'll pay a bit more to have a room and balcony overlooking the river. It's also convenient to downtown. Sharing the same river view, and easy access to downtown, the **Holiday Inn Express Roseburg** (375 W. Harvard Ave., 541/673-7517, $133-157) offers a pool, whirlpool, business center, and some of

the newest rooms in the area. Both these hotels are located just off I-5 Exit 124.

A number of chain hotels are found at I-5 Exit 125, including **Windmill Inn** (1450 NW Mulholland Dr., 541/673-0901 or 800/547-4747, www.windmillinnroseburg.com, $85-99) with comfortable, pet-friendly accommodations with a laundry, restaurant, lounge, and pool. At the same exit, **Best Western Garden Villa Motel** (760 NW Garden Valley Blvd., 541/672-1601 or 800/547-3446, $119-139) has a pool, a business center, and continental breakfast included.

Get away from the freeway ramps at these comfortable lodgings just north of downtown. The flower-bedecked **Rose City Motel** (1142 NE Stephens St., 541/673-8209, www.rosecitymotel.com, $55-65) is an old-fashioned motor court motel that is very well-maintained, with full kitchens and a very friendly welcome. The **Howard Johnson Express** (978 NE Stephens St., 541/673-5082, www.hojo.com, $75-89) is another comfortable older lodging where you don't need to break the bank to have all the perks of an upper-end hotel, including free newspaper, free continental breakfast, and in-room fridge and microwave.

### Camping

For real get-away-from-it-all camping, head up the North Umpqua River where there are many campgrounds. If convenience is what you need, **Armacher County Park** (541/672-4901, $15 tents, $23 RV with hookups) is 5 miles north of town directly beneath I-5 on Exit 129. Although handy, it is not idyllic. **Twin Rivers Vacation Park** (433 Rivers Forks Rd., 541/673-3811, $18-25) is 6 miles out of town off I-5 Exit 125, where the north and south forks of the Umpqua converge. Water, electricity, waste disposal, showers, and a coin-op laundry are available at this 85-site park.

### FOOD

Roseburg is not exactly the fine dining capital of Oregon, but you won't go hungry here. The **Umpqua Valley Farmers Market** (2082

Diamond Lake Blvd., 541/530-6200, 9am-1pm Sat. mid-Apr.-Oct.) takes place in the parking lot of Dutch Brothers Coffee.

The McMenamins brewery empire has an appealing operation at **Roseburg Station** (700 SE Sheridan St., 541/672-1934, 11am-11pm Mon.-Thurs., 11am-midnight Fri.-Sat., noon-10pm Sun., $7-14). The 1912 Southern Pacific Station was purchased and restored while preserving original features like the 16-foot-high ceiling, tongue-and-groove Douglas fir wainscoting, and marble molding. Historical photos and art further recount the depot's storied past. Quality food and microbrews in a setting suitable for families enhance the appeal.

Some of Roseburg's best dining is Italian-style. **◖ Dino's Ristorante Italiano** (404 SE Jackson St., 541/673-0848, 5pm-9pm Tues.-Sat., $15-20) is a cozy family-run spot downtown with decor that's a sprawl of wine cases, travel guides, and cookbooks. The husband-and-wife cooking team spends part of each year in Italy, so the food is about as authentic as you'll find anywhere in southern Oregon.

Famous for its breakfasts, **◖ Brix 527** (527 SE Jackson St., 541/440-4901, 7am-3pm Sun.-Thurs., 7am-9pm Fri., breakfast $8-13, dinner $25-22) is now also open for dinner. At breakfast, Brix 527 gets the basics, like delicious omelets and eggs Benedict, exactly right. At lunch expect soup, salad, and more inventive dishes like grilled bacon-wrapped salmon on saffron rice, and at dinner choose from steaks, fish, and pasta, or perhaps chipotle prawn tacos.

Perhaps downtown's swankiest dining spot is **Blackbird Bar and Grill** (647 SE Jackson St., 541/672-8589, 11:30am-9pm Tues.-Fri., 5pm-9pm Sat., $12-25), with an eclectic menu that ranges from seared polenta and ratatouille to braised lamb shanks and flatiron steak with shallot and red wine reduction.

## INFORMATION

The **Roseburg Visitors and Convention Bureau** (410 SE Spruce St., 541/672-9731 or 800/444-9584, www.visitroseburg.com) has among its brochures a particularly useful drivers guide to historic places.

## GETTING THERE

Buses to and from the **Greyhound** bus depot (835 SE Stephens St., 541/673-5326) connect Roseburg with other cities along the I-5 corridor.

# The North Umpqua River

One of the great escapes into the Cascade Mountains is via the Umpqua Highway, Route 138. This road runs along the part of the North Umpqua River fished by Zane Grey and Clark Gable as well as legions of less-ballyhooed nimrods during steelhead season. The North Umpqua is a premier fishing river full of trout and salmon, as well as a source of excitement for white-water rafters who shoot the rapids. Numerous waterfalls, including 272-foot Watson Falls, feed this great waterway and are found close to the road. Tall timbers line the road through the Umpqua National Forest, and many fine campgrounds are situated within

its confines. Mountain lakes like Toketee Reservoir, Lemolo Lake, and Diamond Lake offer boating and other recreational opportunities. The Umpqua National Forest also boasts challenging yet accessible mountain trails up the flanks of Mount Bailey (8,363 feet) and Mount Thielsen (9,182 feet). And when snow carpets the landscape in winter, you can cross-country ski, snowmobile, and snowcat ski on Mount Bailey free from the crowds at other winter sports areas.

This place is still so untouched primarily because of the rugged terrain. The first road, a crude dirt trail that ran from Roseburg to

# COW CREEK BAND OF THE UMPQUA TRIBE

As you pass Canyonville, along the remote stretch of I-5 between Roseburg and Grants Pass, you'll see the Seven Feathers Casino. It's operated by the Cow Creek Band of the Umpqua Tribe of Native Americans who, like many Oregon tribes, have rallied to regain land that they lost during the pioneer era.

The Cow Creek signed a treaty with the U.S. government in 1853, selling their land in southwestern Oregon for 2.3 cents an acre so that the government could sell it to pioneer settlers for $1.25 an acre. The treaty, which promised health, housing, and education, was ignored by the United States for almost exactly 100 years. The Cow Creek did not receive a reservation, but they stayed in their native area and continued to act as a tribe.

In 1954, the Western Oregon Indian Termination Act terminated federal relations with the Cow Creek and nearly every other tribe in western Oregon. Because the Cow Creek were not notified about their termination until after the act was passed, they sued in the U.S. Court of Claims and eventually won a $1.5 million settlement. The Cow Creek set up an endowment for their settlement money and draw on the interest to further economic development, education, and housing.

The tribe has also been buying back land. In the late 1990s they bought land along Jordan Creek and began clearing out old tires and other garbage that had accumulated there. A watershed assessment pointed to some habitat restoration opportunities, and the tribe set about trying to restore coho salmon and steelhead trout to a stretch of the creek that hadn't seen these fish since 1958, when I-5 was built. After installing weirs that allowed fish to swim through the culverts under I-5, and work on improving water quality and streambank habitat, coho are now spawning in Jordan Creek.

Steamboat, was built in the 1920s. Travelers of the day who wanted to get to the Diamond Lake Resort spent three days traveling this road by car, then had to journey another 20 miles on horseback to reach their final destination. The North Umpqua Road was expanded to Copeland Creek by the Civilian Conservation Corps during the 1930s, but the trips to Diamond and Crater Lakes were still limited to a trail-wise few.

It wasn't until the late 1950s, when President Dwight D. Eisenhower pushed for development of the nation's interstate and state highways, that road improvement began in earnest. Douglas County allocated $2.76 million toward federal matching funds to construct the Umpqua Highway. The road was completed in the summer of 1964, opening up the North Umpqua basin to timber interests, sportspeople, and tourists.

The recreational areas along the North Umpqua fall under the jurisdiction of the **Umpqua National Forest North Umpqua district** (541/496-3532, www.fs.fed.us, based in Glide) and **Diamond Lake district** (541/498-2531, www.fs.fed.us, based near Toketee Falls) and the **Bureau of Land Management** (777 NW Garden Valley Blvd., Roseburg, 541/440-4930, www.blm.gov/or).

## SIGHTS
### Colliding Rivers

Just off Route 138 on the west side of the town of Glide is the site of the **Colliding Rivers.** The Wild and Umpqua Rivers meet head-on in a bowl of green serpentine. The best times to view this spectacle are after winter storms and when spring runoff is high. If the water is low, check out the high-water mark from the Christmas flood of 1964. Water levels from that great inundation were lapping at the parking lot, a chilling reminder that *umpqua* means "thundering water" in Chinook.

Of the many waterfalls along the North Umpqua River, Toketee Falls is the most striking.

## North Umpqua Waterfalls

### GROTTO FALLS

Visitors can get an unusual perspective of **Grotto Falls** because there's a trail in back of this 100-foot cascade. If you venture behind the shimmering water, watch your step because the moss-covered rocks are very slippery. To get here, take Route 138 for 18 miles east of Roseburg to Glide. Follow Little River Road to the Coolwater Campground, and you'll find the turnoff to Forest Service Road 2703 nearby. Take it for 5 miles until you reach the junction of Forest Service Road 2703-150. Proceed down Forest Service Road 2703-150 for another 2 miles until you reach the trailhead. It's only a short hike in to view Grotto Falls.

### SUSAN CREEK FALLS

About 11 miles east of Glide is 50-foot-high **Susan Creek Falls,** whose trailhead sits off Route 138 near the Susan Creek picnic area. A one-mile trail winds through a rainforest-like

setting to the falls. The cascade is bordered on three sides by green mossy rock walls that never see the light of the sun and stay wet 365 days a year. Another 0.25 mile up the trail are the **Indian Mounds.** One of the rites of manhood for Umpqua boys was to fast and pile up stones in hopes of being granted a vision or spiritual powers. Also called the Vision Quest Site, the site still holds stacks of moss-covered stones in an area protected by a fence.

### FALL CREEK FALLS

Four miles east of Susan Creek Falls is **Fall Creek Falls.** Look for the trailhead off Route 138 at Fall Creek. A good walk for families with young children and for older people, the mild one-mile trail goes around and through slabs of bedrock. Halfway up the trail is a lush area called **Job's Garden.** Stay on the Fall Creek Trail and in another 0.5 mile you'll come to the falls. It's a double waterfall with each tier 35-50 feet in height. Back at Job's Garden, you may want to explore the Job's Garden Trail, which leads to the base of columnar basalt outcroppings.

### LITTLE FALLS AND STEAMBOAT FALLS

During fish migration season, it's fun to venture off Route 138 at Steamboat and go up Steamboat Creek Road 38 to see the fish battle two small waterfalls. The first, **Little Falls,** is one mile up the road. It's always exciting to see the fish miraculously wriggle their way up this 10-foot cascade. Four miles farther up Steamboat Creek Road is **Steamboat Falls.** A viewpoint showcases this 30-foot waterfall, but not as many fish try to swim up this one because of the fish ladders nearby.

### JACK FALLS

On Route 138 about 3 miles east of Steamboat is **Jack Falls.** Look for the trailhead sign and follow the trail along the brushy bank of Jack Creek to a series of three closely grouped waterfalls ranging 20-70 feet in height.

### TOKETEE FALLS

The word *toketee* means "graceful" in the Chinook language, and after viewing **Toketee**

Watson Falls drops 272 feet into a ferny glade.

**Falls** plunge over the sheer wall of basalt you'll probably agree it's aptly named. Nineteen miles up Route 138 near the Toketee Ranger Station, this 0.5-mile trail ends at a double waterfall with a combined height of over 150 feet. To get to Toketee Falls, follow Forest Service Road 34 at the west entrance of the ranger station, cross the first bridge, and turn left. There you'll find the trailhead and a parking area.

### WATSON FALLS

On Route 138 take Forest Service Road 37 near the east entrance of the Toketee Ranger Station to reach the trailhead of **Watson Falls,** a 272-foot-high flume of water. A moderate 0.5-mile trail climbs through tall stands of Douglas fir and western hemlock and is complemented by an understory of green salal, Oregon grape, and ferns. A bridge spans the canyon just below the falls, providing outstanding views of this towering cascade. Clamber up the mossy rocks to near the base of the falls and get a face full of the cool billowing spray.

### LEMOLO FALLS

Another waterfall worth a visit is **Lemolo Falls.** *Lemolo* is a Chinook word meaning "wild and untamed," and you'll see that this is the case with this thunderous 100-foot waterfall. To get here, take Lemolo Lake Road off Route 138, then follow Forest Service Roads 2610 and 2610-600 and look for the trailhead sign. The trail is a gentle one-mile path that drops down into the North Umpqua Canyon and passes several small waterfalls on the way to Lemolo Falls.

## Umpqua Hot Springs

The **Umpqua Hot Springs** is mostly unknown and far enough from civilized haunts not to be overused, yet it's accessible enough for those who go in search of it to enjoy. The springs have been developed with wooden pools and a crude lean-to shelter. Weekends tend to attract more visitors, forcing you to wait your turn for a soak. Midweek is generally pretty quiet, though we've encountered some pretty dodgy folks up there these times.

To get here, go north from the Toketee Ranger Station and turn right onto County Road 34, just past the Pacific Power and Light buildings. Proceed down Road 34 past Toketee Lake about 6 miles. When you cross the bridge over Deer Creek, which is clearly signed, you will be a little less than 0.5 mile from the turn-off. The turnoff is Thorn Prairie Road, to the right, which goes 1 mile and ends at a small parking area. Note that in wet weather this road may be impassable, and it is not recommended for low-slung cars in any season. From the parking area, it's 0.5 mile down the blocked road to the hot springs trailhead and another 0.5 mile to the pool.

## SPORTS AND RECREATION
### Hiking

Over 570 miles of trails crisscross the one-million-acre **Umpqua National Forest,** with elevations that range 1,000-9,000 feet. There are hikes to please families and mountain climbers alike. Wildlife and wildflowers, mountain lakes and mountain peaks, old-growth forest

# OAKLAND: VOYAGE INTO THE PAST

Many travelers drive by the exit marked "Oakland" on I-5 joking that maybe they made a wrong turn somewhere and ended up in California. But the curious who venture a few miles off the interstate to explore this National Historic Landmark discover that *this* Oakland is an interesting voyage into Oregon's past. Established in the 1850s, the hamlet today gives little indication of the caprices of fate and fortune it has experienced in its 150-year history. Oakland is noteworthy for leftover touches of refinement from its golden age, which seem almost incongruous against its present-day small-town facade.

Oakland was a stopover point for the main stagecoach line linking Portland and Sacramento until the Oregon and California Railroad came to town in 1872. With these two transportation linkages, Oakland thrived as a trading center for outlying hop fields and prune orchards. In the early 1900s, millions of pounds of dried prunes were shipped all over the world from Oakland. In the 1920s and 1930s, raising turkeys became the prominent industry in the area, and Oakland became the leading turkey-shipping center in the western United States. From the 1940s through the 1960s, the lumber industry dominated the local economy. Today,

livestock ranching, farming, and tourism are the economic mainstays.

While not as commercialized as Jacksonville, its counterpart farther south, Oakland still provides a good place to pull off the interstate and reflect on the passage of years in a onetime boomtown turned rural hamlet.

Old Town Oakland is a good place to start your tour because this is where it all began. An excellent free history and walking-tour pamphlet is available at the city hall (117 3rd St.). The original wooden buildings were destroyed by fires in the 1890s, and most of the brick and stone structures in the historical district date back to this era of reconstruction. The **Oakland Museum** (136 Locust St.) is worth visiting. The exhibit in the back re-creates Oakland during its boom times. There are many antiques stores, art galleries, and curio shops to browse through as well.

**Tolly's** (115 Locust St., 541/459-3796, 11am-3pm Wed.-Thurs. and Sun., 11am-8pm Fri.-Sat., $20-42) is a beautifully preserved restaurant and a great place to stop by for a meal. Be sure to save some room for the homemade desserts, or perhaps something old-fashioned from the soda fountain.

and alpine meadows are some of the attractions visitors see along the way.

If you're camping along the North Umpqua River, many pleasant day hikes are possible on the **North Umpqua Trail.** Beginning near the town of Glide, this thoroughfare parallels the North Umpqua River for most of its 79 miles. Divided into 11 segments from over 3 miles to just under 16 miles in length, the trail leads high into the Cascades and connects with the Pacific Crest Trail as well as many campgrounds. Route 138 affords many access points to the trail.

One segment of the North Umpqua Trail is the one-mile **Panther Trail.** This gentle hike begins near Steamboat at the parking lot of the former ranger station. Many wildflowers are seen late April-early June on the way up

to the old fish hatchery. One flower to look for is the bright-red snow plant, *Sarcodes sanguinea,* which grows beneath Douglas firs and sugar pine trees. Also called the carmine snow flower or snow lily, the snow plant is classified as a saprophyte, a plant that contains no chlorophyll and derives nourishment from decayed materials. Growing 8-24 inches in height, the plant's red flowers are crowded at the crown of the stem.

A five-mile hike that ranges from easy to moderate is found on the south slope of 8,363-foot **Mount Bailey.** Bring plenty of water and good sturdy hiking shoes because the last 0.5 mile of the ascent is steep, with many sharp rocks. To get to the trailhead, take Route 138 to the north entrance of Diamond Lake. Turn

© BILL MCRAE

fishing on the North Umpqua River

onto Forest Service Road 4795 and follow it 5 miles to the junction of Forest Service Road 4795-300. Proceed down 4795-300 for 1 mile until you see the trail marker.

The easy two-mile **Diamond Lake Loop** takes hikers through a mix of lodgepole pine and true fir to Lake Creek, Diamond Lake's only outlet. There are many views of Mount Bailey along the way, as well as some private coves ideal for a swim on hot days. But while the grade is easy, keep in mind that the elevation is nearly a mile high and pace yourself accordingly. To get to the loop, take Forest Service Road 4795 off Route 138 on the north entrance to Diamond Lake and look for the trailhead sign on the west side of the road.

For those who like to climb mountains for reasons other than just because they are there, the **Mount Thielsen Trail** offers a million-dollar view from the top of the mountain. This challenging, scree-covered, five-mile trail winds to the top of Mount Thielsen's spire-pointed 9,182-foot-high volcanic peak. You'll find the trailhead on the east side of Route 138 one mile north of the junction of Route 230.

Bring along water and quick-energy snacks; hiking boots are also recommended due to the sharp volcanic rocks that could easily damage ordinary shoes. Extra care should be taken getting up and down the last 200 feet, which requires hand-over-hand climbing up a steep, crumbly pitch. If you make it to the top, be sure to enter your name in the climbing register found there. Then take a look at the view, which stretches from Mount Shasta to Mount Hood, and forget all the silly preoccupations that plague us mortals.

## Fishing

The North Umpqua has several distinctions. First, it is known as one of the most difficult North American rivers to fish. No boats are permitted for 15 miles in either direction of Steamboat, and no bait or spinners are allowed either. This puts a premium on skillful fly-fishing. You can wade on in and poke around for the best fishing holes on the North Umpqua, one of the few rivers with a summer run of native steelhead—or better yet, hire a guide.

If you want to go with an experienced fishing guide, check out **Summer Run Guide Service** (541/496-3037, www.summerrun.net).

## Rafting

The North Umpqua has increasingly gained popularity with white-water rafters and kayakers. But fishing and floating are not always compatible, so guidelines for boaters and rafters have been established by the Bureau of Land Management and the Umpqua National Forest.

The area around Steamboat has the most restrictions, mainly because of the heavy fishing in the area that boaters would disturb. Be sure to check with the **Forest Service** (541/496-3532) prior to setting out to make sure you are making a legal trip. A good way to get started rafting and avoid the hassle of rules, regulations, and gear is to go along with an experienced white-water guide. These leaders provide the safety equipment, the boats, and the expertise; all you have to do is paddle.

In addition to rafting, inflatable kayak trips are offered by outfitters. Inflatables are easier for the neophyte to handle than the hard-shell type, though these craft expose you to more chills and spills. Whatever your mode of floating the river, expect more than a dozen Class III or IV rapids and plenty of Class IIs, as well as old-growth trees and osprey nests. Best of all, this world-class river is still relatively undiscovered. Spring and summer are the best times to enjoy the North Umpqua, although it's boatable year-round. Boaters are allowed on the river 10am-6pm only, leaving the morning and evening for fish.

**North Umpqua Outfitters** (541/496-3333 or 888/454-9696, www.nuorafting.com) offers raft, kayak, and drift boat trips. Three-hour raft trips are $105 per person; five-hour raft trips with lunch are $125 per person. They also will help you plan a trip that combines rafting and mountain biking.

Other outfitters with similarly price trips include the **Adventure Center** (40 N. Main St., Ashland, 541/482-2897 or 800/444-2819, www.raftingtours.com) and **Orange Torpedo Trips** (209 Merlin Rd., Merlin, 541/479-5061 or 866/479-5061, www.orangetorpedo.com).

## Winter Sports
### SKIING
Located 80 miles east of Roseburg off Route 138 in the central Cascades is Mount Bailey. The experienced skiers at **Cat Ski Mt. Bailey** (800/733-7593, www.catskimtbailey.com, $350 per day) know where the best runs are to be had. Snowcats transport no more than 12 skiers up the mountain from Diamond Lake Resort to the summit of this 8,363-foot peak. Experienced guides then lead small groups down routes that best suit the abilities of each group. The skiing is challenging and should be attempted only by advanced skiers. Open bowls, steep chutes, and tree-lined glaciers are some of the types of terrain encountered during the 3,000-foot drop in elevation back to the resort.

The rates are worth it given the pristine beauty of the area, the dearth of crowds, and the superlative skiing. Attractive packages include overnight lodging in fireside cabins at Diamond Lake Resort as well as an "alpine lunch" of meats, cheeses, vegetables, homemade pie, and coffee served up on the mountain. Only a limited number of skiers can book, so be sure to plan ahead for reservations.

### CROSS-COUNTRY SKIING
Over 56 miles of designated Nordic trails are found in the Diamond and Lemolo Lakes area along the upper reaches of Route 138. Some of the trails are groomed, and all of them are clearly marked by blue trail signs. Contact the **Umpqua National Forest** (Diamond Lake Ranger District, 541/498-2531, www.fs.usda.gov/umpqua) to request maps and information on these trails.

The **Diamond Lake Resort** (Diamond Lake, 541/793-3333 or 800/733-7593, www.diamondlake.net, 8am-5pm daily) rents skis and snowshoes.

### TUBING AND SNOWBOARDING
If you ski the bunny hill, you might enjoy inner-tubing or snowboarding near **Diamond Lake Resort** (Diamond Lake, 541/793-3333 or 800/733-7593, www.diamondlake.net). A rope tow takes "tubers" to the top of the hill 9am-5pm weekends for nonstop thrills and spills on the way back down. The hill has a ticket system similar to other ski lifts, with full-day, half-day, and two-hour passes available. The tubing and snowboarding hill is located at the Hilltop Shop. The $10 entry fee includes an inner tube, a tow rope, and a cable clip. Uphill tows are $0.50.

### SNOWMOBILING
Approximately 133 miles of designated motorized snow trails are concentrated around the Lemolo and Diamond Lakes area. The trails are usually open in late November, as snow accumulation permits. Many of these trails are groomed on a regular basis, and all are clearly marked by orange trail signs and

The Steamboat Inn is famed for its fishing access and its fine dining.

diamond-shaped trail blazes pegged up on trees above the snowline. Diamond Lake Resort is a hub of snowmobiling activity; they rent snow machines and can advise you on trails.

One of the more exotic runs is into Crater Lake National Park. Snowmobiles and all-terrain vehicles (ATVs) must register at the north entrance of the park and stay on the trail. The trail climbs about 10 miles from the park gates to the north rim of the lake. Be aware that the mountain weather here can change suddenly, creating dangerous subzero temperatures and whiteout conditions. Also, watch for Nordic skiers and other people sometimes found on motorized vehicle trails.

## ACCOMMODATIONS

The number of lodgings on the North Umpqua River is limited to a few properties that range from rustic quarters to full-service resorts.

About four miles east of Idleyld Park is the **Dogwood Motel** (28866 N. Umpqua Hwy., Idleyld Park, 541/496-3403, www. dogwoodmotel.com, $70-75). Here you'll find clean modern units, some with kitchenettes, on tidy well-kept grounds.

The **(** **Steamboat Inn** (42705 N. Umpqua Hwy., Steamboat, 541/498-2230 or 800/840-8825, www.thesteamboatinn. com, Mar.-Dec., $185-300) is the premier dining and accommodation property on the North Umpqua, situated in the middle of a stretch of 31 miles of premium fly-fishing turf. The inn's rooms and cabins are extremely popular, so reservations are a must. It's an ideal getaway from civilization, near the hiking trails, waterfalls, and fishing holes for which the Umpqua is famous. Lodging is in handsomely furnished riverside cabins, cottages, and suites; a number of three-bedroom ranch-style houses are also available. The inn serves breakfast, lunch, and dinner to its guests; nonguests may also dine.

Near the summit of the Cascade Mountains about 75 miles east of Roseburg and 13 miles from Diamond Lake is **Lemolo Lake Resort**

(2610 Birds Point Rd., Idleyld Park, 541/643-0750, www.lemololakeresort.com, cabins $150-250, hotel rooms $90-100), a more modest operation. Formed by a Pacific Power and Light dam, Lemolo Lake has good fishing for German brown trout as well as kokanee salmon, eastern brook trout, and rainbow trout. The lake is sheltered from wind by gently sloping ridges, and there are many coves and sandy beaches along the 8.3 miles of shoreline. Waterskiing is permitted on the lake. Boats and canoes can be rented, and many miles of snowmobiling and cross-country skiing trails are nearby. The resort has both housekeeping and standard cabins as well as basic hotel rooms.

**Diamond Lake Resort** (Diamond Lake, 541/793-3333 or 800/733-7593, www.diamondlake.net) is a rustic mountain resort with enough modern amenities to suit the tenderfoot in any season. It offers lodging, restaurants, groceries, a service station, a laundry, and showers. Cabins with one queen bed or two twins start at $109; lodge and motel rooms start at $99. Lodgings are popular as base camps for a Crater Lake excursion. Mountain bikes, paddleboats, kayaks, canoes, and fishing boats as well as an equestrian center keep you out of the modest accommodations and busy enjoying the spectacular surroundings.

# CAMPING
## Little River Campgrounds
If the thought of a campground with good shade trees and a waterfall with a swimming hole sounds idyllic, head for **Cavitt Creek Falls** (Bureau of Land Management, 541/440-4930, May-late Oct., $8). To get there, head east of Roseburg on Route 138 to Glide, take Little Creek Road (County Road 17) for 7 miles, then continue 3 miles down Cavitt Creek Road. Ten campsites with picnic tables and grills are provided, with piped water, vault toilets, and firewood available on the premises.

Another campsite 5 miles up Little River Road is **Wolf Creek** (North Umpqua Ranger District, 541/496-3532, mid-May-late Oct., $15), which features eight sites for tents and RVs (up to 30 feet) and three tent-only sites.

Picnic tables, grills, vault toilets, and piped water are provided.

An easy way to keep your cool is at **Coolwater** (North Umpqua Ranger District, 541/496-3532, mid-May-late Oct., $10). Seven tent sites and sites for RVs (up to 24 feet) with picnic tables and grills are available; vault toilets and well water from a hand pump are also on the grounds. To get here, follow Little River Road 15 miles out of Glide. There are many good hiking trails nearby, including **Grotto Falls, Wolf Creek Nature Trail,** and **Wolf Creek Falls Trail.**

One of the best deals on the Little River is at **White Creek** (North Umpqua Ranger District, 541/496-3532, mid-May-late Sept., $10), a small four-site campground that accommodates tents and RVs. Picnic tables and grills are provided, and piped water and vault toilets are available. Situated on the confluence of White Creek and Little River, a good beach and shallow water provide excellent swimming for children. To get here, take Little Creek Road 17 miles to Red Butte Road and proceed 1 mile down Red Butte Road to the campground.

Tucked away on the upper reaches of the Little River at an elevation of 3,200 feet is **Lake in the Woods** (North Umpqua Ranger District, 541/496-3532, June-late Oct., $10). You'll find 11 sites for tents and RVs (up to 16 feet), with picnic tables, grills, vault toilets, and hand-pumped water in a campground set along the shore of the four-acre artificial Little Lake in the Woods. Motorized craft are not permitted in this eight-foot-deep pond. Two good hikes nearby are to **Hemlock Falls** and **Yakso Falls.** To get here, head 20 miles up Little River Road to the end of the pavement; proceed another 7 miles until you reach the campground.

## North Umpqua River Campgrounds
Set along the bank of the North Umpqua River 15 miles east of Roseburg a little ways north of Route 138 is **Whistler's Bend** (541/673-4863, $15), a Douglas County park. Picnic tables and grills are provided at this county park,

© BILL MCRAE

**Diamond Lake is a popular boating destination in summer.**

as are piped water, flush toilets, and showers. The fishing is good here, and even though it's fairly close to town, it doesn't usually get too crowded.

About 30 miles east of Route 138 is **Susan Creek** (Bureau of Land Management, 541/440-4930, May-late Oct., $14). This campground has 31 sites for tents and RVs (up to 20 feet) with picnic tables and grills. Flush toilets, piped water, and firewood are also available. Situated in a grove of old-growth Douglas fir and sugar pine next to the North Umpqua River, the campground is enhanced by the presence of a fine beach and swimming hole.

Within easy access of great fishing (fly-angling only), rafting, and hiking, **Bogus Creek** (North Umpqua Ranger District, 541/496-3532, May 1-Oct. 31, $15) offers you the real thing. Here you'll find 5 tent sites and 10 sites for tents or RVs (up to 30 feet) with picnic tables and grills. Flush toilets, iodinated water, and gray wastewater sumps are available. As the campground is a major launching point for white-water expeditions and within a few miles

of Fall Creek Falls and Job's Garden Geological Area, it's good to get here early to make sure you get a campsite.

About 38 miles east of Roseburg on Route 138 near Steamboat and good fly-fishing is **Canton Creek** (North Umpqua Ranger District, 541/496-3532, May-mid-Oct., $10). Take Steamboat Creek Road off Route 138 and proceed 400 yards to the campground. This campground features 12 sites for tents and RVs (up to 22 feet) with the standard picnic tables and grills, plus piped water, flush toilets, and gray wastewater sumps.

**Horseshoe Bend** (North Umpqua Ranger District, 541/496-3532, mid-May-late Sept., $115) is 10 miles east of Steamboat. There are 34 sites for tents and RVs (up to 35 feet) with picnic tables and grills. Flush toilets, piped water, gray wastewater sumps, a laundry, and a general store are also available. Situated in the middle of a big bend of the North Umpqua covered with old-growth Douglas firs and sugar pines, this is a popular base camp for rafting and fishing enthusiasts.

### Diamond Lake Campgrounds

Several campgrounds are in the vicinity of beautiful 5,200-foot-high Diamond Lake; boating, fishing, swimming, bicycling, and hiking are among the popular recreational options. The trout fishing is particularly good in the early summer, and there are also excellent hikes into the Mount Thielsen Wilderness, Crater Lake National Park, and Mount Bailey areas. While no reservations are technically necessary, these campgrounds can fill up fast, so it's always a good idea to book a space ahead of time (877/444-6777 or www.recreation.gov). For general information, contact the **Diamond Lake Ranger District** (541/498-2531, www. fs.usda.gov/umpqua).

Although Route 138 twists and turns most of the 80 miles from Roseburg to Diamond Lake, many people head straight for **Broken Arrow** (mid-May-Labor Day, $15). This 142-site campground with standard picnic tables and grills has plenty of room for tents and RVs (up to 30 feet); flush toilets, piped water, and gray wastewater sumps are available.

The next campground bears the name of its raison d'être, **Diamond Lake** (May 15-Oct. 31, $16-27). Here you'll find 160 campsites for tents and RVs (up to 22 feet) with picnic tables and grills. Piped water, flush toilets, and firewood are also available. Numerous hiking trails lead from the campground, including the Pacific Crest National Scenic Trail. Boat docks, launching facilities, and rentals are nearby at **Diamond Lake Resort** (Diamond Lake, 541/793-3333 or 800/733-7593, www. diamondlake.net).

On the east shore of Diamond Lake is **Thielsen View** (mid-May-mid-Oct., $15). It features 60 sites for tents and RVs (up to 30 feet) with picnic tables and grills. Piped water, vault toilets, gray wastewater sumps, and a boat ramp are also available. As the name implies, this campground has picturesque views of Mount Thielsen.

## FOOD

Make a reservation at the outstanding **◖ Steamboat Inn** (42705 N. Umpqua Hwy., 541/498-2230 or 800/840-8825, www. thesteamboatinn.com, 8am-9pm daily) to dine on main dishes of beef, fish, poultry, lamb, or pork served with fresh vegetables and homemade bread. Considered one of the top dining experiences in the state, the Steamboat also has a wide selection of Oregon wines. The prix fixe Evening Dinner ($50) is served nightly, and Winemaker's Dinners (Mar.-mid-June, $90) are scheduled frequently during the summer and on weekends the rest of the season. The chef can also accommodate any food allergies, strong dislikes, and vegetarian diets. Reservations for dinner are required.

# Crater Lake

High in the Cascades lies the crown jewel of Oregon, Crater Lake, the country's deepest at 1,943 feet. It glimmers like a polished sapphire in a setting created by a volcano that blew its top and collapsed thousands of years ago. Crater Lake's extraordinary hues are produced by the depth and clarity of the water and its ability to absorb all the colors of the spectrum except the shortest wavelengths, blue and violet, which are scattered skyward. Kodak used to send their apologies along with customers' photographs of Crater Lake—they thought they had goofed on the processing, so unbelievable is the blue of the water.

In addition to a 33-mile rim loop around the crater, the park, established in 1902, also features 229 campsites, dozens of hiking trails, and boat tours on the lake itself. Admission to the park is $10 per vehicle or $5 per bicycle.

If you're seeing Crater Lake for the first time, drive into the park from the north for the most dramatic perspective. After crossing through a pumice desert you climb up to higher elevations overlooking the lake. In

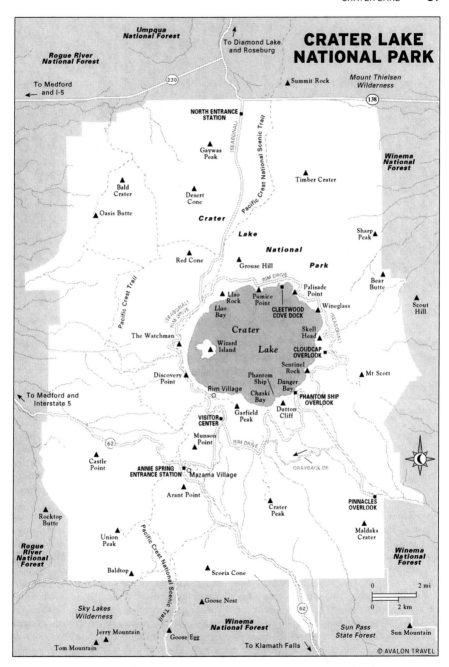

# CRATER LAKE NATIONAL PARK

Umpqua National Forest

Rogue River National Forest

To Diamond Lake and Roseburg

Mount Thielsen Wilderness

▲ Summit Rock

To Medford and I-5

230

138

NORTH ENTRANCE STATION

Winema National Forest

▲ Gaywas Peak

(SEASONAL)

Pacific Crest National Scenic Trail

▲ Timber Crater

▲ Bald Crater

▲ Desert Cone

*Crater*

▲ Oasis Butte

*Lake*

Sharp Peak ▲

*National*

▲ Red Cone

▲ Grouse Hill

*Park*

RIM DRIVE

Palisade Point ▲

Bear Butte ▲

Pacific Crest Trail

(SEASONAL) RIM DRIVE

▲ Llao Rock

Pumice Point

▲ Wineglass

Scout Hill ▲

Llao Bay

CLEETWOOD COVE DOCK

The Watchman

Skell Head ▲

(SEASONAL)

*Crater*

*Lake*

CLOUDCAP OVERLOOK

▲ Wizard Island

Discovery Point

Sentinel Rock ▲

▲ Mt Scott

Phantom Ship

*Danger Bay*

Rim Village ○

*Chaski Bay*

PHANTOM SHIP OVERLOOK

VISITOR CENTER ■

▲ Garfield Peak

Dutton Cliff

To Medford and Interstate 5

Munson Point

RIM DRIVE

62

▲ Castle Point

GRAYBACK DR

ANNIE SPRING ENTRANCE STATION ○

Mazama Village

▲ Arant Point

PINNACLES OVERLOOK

▲ Rocktop Butte

▲ Union Peak

▲ Crater Peak

▲ Maldaks Crater

*Rogue River National Forest*

Pacific Crest National Scenic Trail

*Winema National Forest*

▲ Baldtop

▲ Scoria Cone

0        2 mi

0        2 km

*Sky Lakes Wilderness*

▲ Goose Nest

62

▲ Jerry Mountain ▲

▲ Goose Egg

*Winema National Forest*

*Sun Pass State Forest*

▲ Sun Mountain

▲ Tom Mountain

To Klamath Falls

© AVALON TRAVEL

Wizard Island
© BILL MCRAE

contrast to this subdued approach, the blueness and size of the lake can hit you with a suddenness that stops all thought. On a clear day, you can peer south across Crater Lake and discern the snowy eminence of Mount Shasta over 100 miles away in California.

## Geology

Geologically speaking, the name *Crater Lake* is a misnomer. Technically, Crater Lake lies in a caldera, which is produced when the center of a volcano caves in on itself; in this case, the cataclysm occurred 6,600 years ago with the destruction of formerly 12,000-foot-high Mount Mazama.

Klamath Native American legend has it that Mount Mazama was the home of Llao, king of the underworld. The chief of the world above was Skell, who sometimes would stand on Mount Shasta, 100 miles to the south. A fierce battle between these two gods took place, a time marked by great explosions, thunder, and lightning. Burning ash fell from the sky, igniting the forest, and molten rivers of

lava gushed 35 miles down the mountainside, burying Native American villages. For a week the night sky was lit by the flames of the great confrontation.

The story climaxes with Skell's destruction of Llao's throne, as the mountain collapsed on itself and sealed Llao beneath the surface, never again to frighten the people and destroy their homes. Although the lake became serene and beautiful as the caldera filled with water, the Klamaths believed that only punishment awaited those who foolishly gazed upon the sacred battleground of the gods.

The aftereffects of this great eruption can still be seen. Huge drifts of ash and pumice hundreds of feet deep were deposited over a wide area up to 80 miles away. The pumice deserts to the north of the lake and the deep ashen canyons to the south are the most dramatic examples. So thick and widespread is the pumice that water percolates through too rapidly for plants to survive, creating reddish pockets of bleakness in the otherwise green forest. The eerie gray hoodoos in the southern canyons were created by hot gases bubbling up through the ash, hardening it into rocklike towers. These formations have withstood centuries of erosion by water that has long since washed away the loosely packed ash, creating the steep canyons visible today.

**Wizard Island,** a large cinder cone that rises 760 feet above the surface of the lake, offers evidence of volcanic activity since the caldera's formation. The **Phantom Ship,** in the southeastern corner, is a much older feature.

The lake is confined by walls of multicolored lava that rise 500-2,000 feet above the water. Although Crater Lake is fed entirely by snow and rain, the lake does contain a small amount of salts from surrounding rocks, but the salty water is replaced by purer rain and snow. The level of the lake fluctuates only 1-3 feet per year as evaporation and seepage keep it remarkably constant.

Another surprise is that while Crater Lake often records the coldest temperatures in the Cascades, the lake itself has only frozen over once since records have been kept. The surface of the lake can warm up to the 60°F mark during the summer. The deeper water stays around 38°F, although scientists have discovered 66°F hot spots 1,400 feet below the lake's surface.

Rainbow trout and kokanee (a landlocked salmon) were introduced to the lake many years ago by humans. The rainbow can grow up to 25 inches long, feeding mainly on the kokanee; the kokanee do not exceed 15 inches. Some types of mosses and green algae grow more than 400 feet below the lake's surface, a world record for these freshwater species. Another distinction is Crater Lake's selection as the purest lake in the world by scientists who determined in 1997 that the water's clarity extended down 142 feet.

# ◖ CRATER LAKE NATIONAL PARK
## Visitors Center
The **visitors center** (9am-5pm daily early Apr.-early Nov., 10am-4pm daily early Nov.-early Apr., closed Christmas day), is located below Rim Village near park headquarters and can provide information, maps, and publications as well as backcountry permits and first aid. If the lake is socked in by lousy weather, you can see it anyway: Excellent films about Crater Lake are shown in the center's theater every half hour and by special arrangement. For information about weather and activities at Crater Lake, visit www.nps.gov/crla or call 541/594-3000.

The **original visitors center** (9:30am-5pm daily late May-late Sept.) is on the rim. A rock stairway behind the small building leads to Sinnott Memorial and one of the best views of the lake. It is perched on a rock outcropping where accompanying interpretive placards help you identify the surrounding formations as well as flora and fauna. As you drive north from Rim Village, a few miles on you'll notice brown earth that spread out from the last major eruption.

## Boat Tours
There are over 100 miles of hiking trails in the park, yet only one leads down to the lake itself. This is because the 1.1-mile-long Cleetwood Trail is the only part of the caldera's steep avalanche-prone slope that is safe enough for passage. The trail drops 700 feet in elevation and is recommended only for those in good physical condition. There is no other way to get to **Cleetwood Cove dock,** located at the end of the trail, where the **Crater Lake boat tours** (541/830-8700) begin.

There are two types of boat tours. Narrated excursions depart on the half hour 9:30am-3:30pm July-mid-September ($35 adults, $21 children ages 3-11) and cruise counterclockwise around the perimeter of the lake. These tours do not stop at Wizard Island. Twice daily, at 9:30am and 12:30pm, a cruise departs with a stop at Wizard Island ($45 adults, $27 children). You can elect to hike to the summit of the island and return on the later boat.

Allow one hour from Rim Village to drive 12 miles to Cleetwood trailhead and hike down to the boat's departure point. Dress warmly because it's cooler on the lake than on terra firma.

A limited number of boat tour tickets are

available by reservation at www.craterlakelodges.com. The rest of the tickets are sold first-come, first-served at the Cleetwood Trail ticket kiosk.

## Hiking

July and August are the most popular months for hiking. Colorful flowers and mild weather greet the summer throngs. One of the best places to view the mid-July flora is on the **Castle Crest Wildflower Trail.** The trailhead to this 0.5-mile loop trail is 0.5 mile from the park headquarters. Stop there for directions to the trailhead as well as a self-guided trail booklet that tells you about the ponderosa pine, Shasta red fir, mountain hemlock, lodgepole pine, and rabbitbrush along the trail. Wildlife in the area includes elk, deer, foxes, pikas, marmots, and a variety of birds. Peak wildflower season is usually around the last two weeks of July.

A suitable challenge of brawn and breath is the **Garfield Peak Trail.** The trailhead to this imposing ridge is just east of Crater Lake Lodge. It is a steep climb up the 1.7-mile trail, but the wildflower displays of phlox, Indian paintbrush, and lupine, as well as frequent sightings of eagles and hawks, give ample opportunity for you to stop and catch your breath. The highlight of the hike is atop Garfield Peak, which provides a spectacular view of Crater Lake 1,888 feet below.

A new trail leads from the Pinnacles Road, just off the East Rim Drive southeast of the Phantom Ship overlook, to **Plaikni Falls,** a pretty cascade that rolls down a glacier-carved cliff. The 1.1-mile trail is along a well-graded, wheelchair-accessible dirt path.

## Winter Sports

When snow buries the area in the wintertime, services and activities are cut to a minimum. However, many cross-country skiers, snowshoe enthusiasts, and winter campers enjoy this solitude. Park rangers lead **snowshoe hikes** (weather permitting) at 1pm on weekends, daily during Christmas week. Ski and snowshoe rentals are available at Rim Village.

Winter trekkers should be aware that there are no groomed cross-country trails, so it's imperative to inquire about trail, avalanche,

road, and weather conditions at the visitor center. Circumnavigating the lake, which is visited by frequent snowstorms, takes 2-3 days, even in good weather. Only skilled winter hikers should attempt this 33-mile route that requires a compass and maps to traverse unmarked routes and avalanche paths.

Prior to setting out on any extended backcountry journey, pick up a permit and some free advice at the visitors center. You might also inquire about a hike to the top of **Mount Scott** (8,926 feet), the highest peak in the area. Lake views and perspectives on 12 Cascade peaks are potential rewards at the end of the 2.5-mile trek.

## Trolley Tours

Passengers can take two-hour round-trip tours on newly built but historically designed **trolley cars** (541/882-1896, www.craterlaketrolley.com, tours depart 10am-3pm on the hour July-early Oct., $25 adults, $15 children ages 5-13) along Rim Drive, with several stops at scenic viewpoints. The natural gas-powered trolleys are ADA-compliant and feature commentary by a guide. Purchase tickets at the Community House at Rim Village, near the Crater Lake Lodge.

## Accommodations and Food

One of the nicest things about 183,180-acre Crater Lake National Park is that it's not very developed. Lodging and services are concentrated on the southern edge of the lake at **Rim Village;** the exact opening and closing dates for services changes from year to year, depending on the snowpack. (Note: The park received 649 inches of snow—more than 54 feet—during the winter of 2010-2011!) In general, restaurants and information services are open mid-May-mid-October, with the exception of the **Rim Village Cafe,** which is open year-round. The café serves traditional breakfasts, and lunch and dinner offerings include salads, grab-and-go sandwiches, pizzas, and assorted snacks. A small grocery section in the adjoining gift shop sells basic foodstuffs and beverages in case you've run out of peanut butter or beer.

Crater Lake Lodge

The 71-room ◖ **Crater Lake Lodge** (541/830-8700, www.craterlakelodges.com, late May-mid-Oct., $164-225, lakefront rooms extra) is situated on the rim south of the Sinnott Overlook and is hewn of indigenous wood and stone. The massive lobby boasts a picture window on the lake and has decor echoing its 1915 origins. The stone fireplace is large enough to walk into and serves as a gathering spot on chilly evenings. Many of the rooms have expansive views of the lake below. Others face out toward upper Klamath Lake and Mount Shasta, 100 miles away in California.

Amid all the amenities of a national park hotel, it's nice to be reminded of the past by such touches as antique wallpaper and old-fashioned bathtubs (rooms 401 and 201 offer views of the lake from claw-foot tubs). This marriage of past and present in such a prime location has proven so popular that it's imperative to reserve many months in advance. The 72-seat **dining room** (7am-10:30am, 11:30am-2:30pm, and 5pm-10pm daily, early June-mid-Sept., $21-34) features Pacific Northwest cuisine in a classic setting, and gives preference to reservations made by hotel guests.

Seven miles south of the rim is another cluster of services called Mazama Village. At the **Cabins at Mazama Village** (541/830-8700, www.craterlakelodges.com, late May-late Sept., $140), each guest room features two queen beds and a bath, and two cabins are designed for wheelchair access. Be sure to call ahead for reservations.

Also in Mazama Village, the **Annie Creek Restaurant** (7am-10:30am and 11:30am-9pm daily, early June-mid-Sept., dinner $11-25) serves American style comfort foods, including burgers, pot roast, fried chicken, and vegetarian lasagna.

## Camping

**Mazama Village Campground** (reservations at www.craterlakelodges.com, early June-late Sept., $21 tents, $29-35 RVs), seven miles south of the rim, has over 200 sites, restrooms with coin-operated showers, and a dump station.

**Lost Creek Campground** (mid-July-early Oct., $10 tents), on the eastern section of Rim Drive, has 16 sites, water, and pit toilets. Foot traffic in the backcountry is light, so you can set up camp wherever you like in the remote areas surrounding Crater Lake.

### Getting There

The only year-round access to Crater Lake is from the south via Route 62. To reach Crater Lake from Grants Pass, head for Gold Hill and take Route 234 until it meets Route 62. As you head up Route 62 you might spot roadside snow poles in anticipation of the onset of winter. This highway makes a horseshoe bend through the Cascades, starting at Medford and ending 20 miles north of Klamath Falls. The northern route via Route 138 (Roseburg to U.S. 97, south of Beaver Marsh) is usually closed by snow mid-October-July. The tremendous snowfall also closes 33-mile-long Rim Drive, although portions are opened when conditions permit. Rim Drive is generally opened to motorists around the same time as the northern entrance to the park.

## CRATER LAKE HIGHWAY (HWY. 62)

Some of the locals who live near the Crater Lake Highway sport bumper stickers on their vehicles that read "I Survived Highway 62." The challenges of successfully navigating this precipitous and circuitous thoroughfare, with its horrific winter weather and slow-moving summer crowds, help give it a killer reputation. Snow can sometimes get deep enough on the upper reaches that 15-foot-tall snow poles lining the roadbed are rendered useless in helping the snowplows navigate. In these cases, the crews can only locate the road by means of a radio transmitter, embedded in steel cable, which emits a signal.

Even so, there always seems to be traffic on this winding conduit between Crater Lake and southern Oregon. This isn't surprising when you consider the scenic appeal of the Rogue River and the Cascade Mountains. And then there's fishing. The salmon runs on the Rogue River are second in size only to the ones on the Columbia. Nearly

three million fish are reared and released into the Rogue from the Cole Rivers Fish Hatchery, 153 miles from the mouth of the Rogue. With swimming, boating, and rafting opportunities, the Rogue River is indeed tempting, and you too will be taking to the hills along Route 62.

The following contacts can help plan your foray into the Rogue River National Forest: **Prospect Ranger Station** (541/560-3400), **Rogue River National Forest Service** (3040 Biddle Rd., Medford, 541/618-2200), and **Travel Oregon** (http://traveloregon.com).

### Hiking

Many choice hikes are found along the 50-mile stretch of the Rogue River Trail from Lost Creek Lake to the river's source at Boundary Springs, just inside Crater Lake National Park. Lofty waterfalls, deep gushing gorges, and a natural bridge are all easily accessible. Those interested in more than just a short walk from the parking lot to the viewpoint can design hikes of 2-18 miles with or without an overnight stay. Travelers with two cars can arrange shuttles to avoid having to double back.

One of the more scenic recreation spots is owned by Boise Cascade, a timber conglomerate. Boise Cascade has constructed a botanical nature trail system through its land to a series of three waterfalls in an impressive rock-choked section of the Rogue River called the Avenue of the Giant Boulders.

The largest of the three waterfalls is **Mill Creek Falls,** which plunges 173 feet down into the river. Signs along the highway and Mill Creek Drive (formerly the old Crater Lake Highway), a scenic loop out of the community of Prospect, direct visitors to the trailhead. A large map further details the trail routes. The trail is short but steep; wear shoes you don't mind getting wet and that have good traction, as you may have to scramble over some of the boulders and wade through some small ponds along the way.

A particularly wild section of the river is found at **Takelma Gorge.** Located 1 mile from River Bridge Campground on the upper Rogue River, the trail offers vistas of sharp foaming bends in the river with logs jammed at crazy angles on the rocks, along with ferns growing in the mist of the waterfalls. Although the river's course is rugged, the grade on the trail is gentle.

Even if you're in a hurry, you should take 15 minutes to get out of your car and stretch your legs at the **Natural Bridge.** Located 0.25 mile from Natural Bridge Campground, 1 mile west of Union Creek on Route 62, here the Rogue River drops into a lava tube and disappears from sight, only to emerge a little way downstream. A short paved path takes you to an artificial bridge that fords this unique section of the river. Several placards along the way explain the formation of the Natural Bridge and other points of interest.

Just outside of Union Creek on Route 62 is the spectacular **Rogue River Gorge.** At this narrowest point on the river, the action of the water has carved out a deep chasm in the rock. A short trail with several well-placed overlooks follows the rim of the gorge. Green mossy walls, logjams, and a frothy torrent of water are all clearly visible from the trail. Informative placards discuss curiosities like the living stump and the potholes carved in the lava rock by pebbles and the action of the water.

Another short hike for hurried motorists is **National Creek Falls.** An easy 0.5-mile walk down a trail bordered by magnificent Douglas firs leads to this tumultuous cascade. To get here, take Route 230 to Forest Service Road 6530. Follow the road until you reach the trailhead, marked by a sign.

A two-mile hike down a cool and shady trail takes you to the source of the mighty Rogue River—**Boundary Springs.** Situated just inside Crater Lake National Park, it's a great place for a picnic. About one mile down the path from the trailhead, hang a left at the fork to get to Boundary Springs. Once at the springs, you'll discover small cataracts rising out of the jumbled volcanic rock that's densely covered with moss and other vegetation. Despite the temptation to get a closer look, the vegetation here is extremely fragile, so refrain from walking on the moss. To get here, take Route 230 north from Route 62 to the crater rim viewpoint, where parking can be found on the left-hand side of the road.

To enjoy the golden hues of larches and aspens in the fall, take Route 62 from Medford and turn east onto Route 140. En route, you might stop at Fish Lake or Lake of the Woods resorts. From here you can take scenic Westside Road to Fort Klamath; Crater Lake lies a scant 6 miles from here.

## Accommodations

The accommodations you'll find on Route 62 are rustic and simple, catering mainly to anglers and lovers of the great outdoors.

Rooms at the **Maple Leaf Motel** (20717 Rte. 62, Shady Cove, 541/878-2169, www.maple-leafmotel.org, $80-95) come equipped with a microwave, a toaster oven, a small fridge, cable TV, and a picnic and barbecue area to grill the day's catch or some burgers if the fish weren't biting. The **Royal Coachman Motel** (21906 Rte. 62, Shady Cove, 541/878-2481, www.roy-alcoachmanmotel.com, $59-76) has kitchenettes, cable TV, and HBO. The more expensive rooms have lovely decks that overlook the river.

The **Prospect Hotel and Motel** (391 Mill Creek Rd., Prospect, 541/560-3664 or 800/944-6490, www.prospecthotel.com, historic hotel rooms $140-205 including breakfast, motel rooms $90-145) gives you a choice between something old and something new. The hotel, built in 1889 and listed on the National Register of Historic Places, has several small but comfortable guest rooms with baths. The rooms are named after local residents and famous people who have stayed at the hotel, including Zane Grey, Teddy Roosevelt, and Jack London. Because the hotel is small and old, no children, smoking, or pets are permitted. The adjacent motel features clean, spacious, and modern units, with some kitchenettes available. Pets are welcome in the motel.

Not far away from Prospect on the Crater Lake Highway is the **Union Creek Resort** (56484 Hwy. 62, Prospect, 866/560-3565, www.unioncreekoregon.com). Built in the early 1930s, the Union Creek is listed on the National Register of Historic Places. Open year-round, it has rooms available in your choice of the original lodge, simple cabins with bathrooms, or housekeeping cabins with kitchens and bathrooms. The lodge rooms ($60-68), paneled in knotty pine, have washbasins; guests share the bathrooms down the hall. The stone fireplace in the lobby was built of opalized wood from Lakeview, Oregon. The sleeping cabins with baths range $110-165. The vacation rental housekeeping cabins sleep up to 10 and range $220-265. If you like rustic cabins and lodges, the Union Creek is the real deal. The **Union Creek Country Store,** located at the resort, carries groceries and other essential items. Fishing licenses and Sno-Park permits can also be purchased here.

## Camping

For those who like roughing it in style with all of the perks of an RV, **Rogue River RV Park** (218005 Hwy. 62, Shady Cove, 541/878-2404) is right on the banks of the Rogue River about 23 miles north of Medford on Route 62.

Five miles below Lost Creek Lake on Route 62 at 1,476 feet in elevation is **Rogue Elk County Park** (Jackson County Parks and Recreation, 541/776-7001, mid-Apr.-mid-Oct., $18, $21 with electricity and water hookups). This campground features sites for tents and RVs (up to 28 feet) with piped water, showers, and flush toilets on the premises. The kids will enjoy swimming in Elk Creek, which, in addition to being adjacent to the campground, is warmer and safer than the Rogue River; a playground adds to the fun. The park has a $3 per vehicle day-use fee.

Along the shore of Lost Creek Lake is **Joseph Stewart State Park** (35251 Rte. 62, Trail, 541/560-3334, www.oregonstateparks.org, Mar.-Oct., $17-20). This large campground is set on a big grassy field above the reservoir and has all the usual state park amenities. Bike paths, a beach, and barbecue grills make this a family-friendly locale, if not exactly getting away from it all. Boat-launching facilities for Lost Creek Lake are located nearby, and eight miles of hiking trails and bike paths crisscross the park. Lost Creek Lake also has a marina, a beach, and boat rentals.

If you want to get away from the highway, head for **Abbott Creek** (Rogue National Forest, Prospect Ranger Station, 541/560-3400, late May-Oct., $12), but bear in mind that this is where off-highway vehicle riders come to play. One of the few backwoods camps in the area that has potable water, it's 7 miles northeast of the town of Prospect on Route 62 and 3 miles down Forest Service Road 68.

Set along the woodsy bank of Union Creek where it merges with the upper Rogue River is **Union Creek** (Rogue National Forest, Prospect Ranger Station, 541/560-3400, late May-Oct., $12). Located 11 miles northeast of Prospect, you'll find 78 sites for tents and RVs (up to 16 feet) with picnic tables, grills, piped water, and vault toilets. Many fine hikes on the Rogue River Trail are within close proximity of the campground.

Half a mile past Union Creek Campground on Route 62 is **Farewell Bend** (Rogue National Forest, Prospect Ranger Station, 541/560-3400, late May-early Sept., $16), the best-appointed of the Upper Rogue campgrounds. Near the junction of Route 62 and Route 230, the camp has 61 sites for tents and RVs (up to 22 feet) with picnic tables and grills. Piped water and flush toilets are also within the campground boundaries. This campground is situated along the banks of the Upper Rogue near the Rogue River Gorge Trail.

A nice little campground tucked off the highway yet fairly close to the Rogue River and Crater Lake National Park is **Huckleberry Campground** (Rogue National Forest, Prospect Ranger Station, 541/560-3400, late May-Oct. weather permitting, free, no water). To get here, go about 18 miles northeast of Prospect on Route 62 and then 4 miles down Forest Service Road 60. You'll find 25 sites for tents and RVs (up to 21 feet) with picnic tables and grills. This campground is at an elevation of 5,400 feet, so be sure to have the proper gear to ensure a comfortable visit.

## Food

The best restaurants along Highway 62 are at the old-fashioned resorts in Prospect and Union Creek. The dining room at the **Prospect Hotel** (391 Mill Creek Rd., Prospect, 541/560-3664 or 800/944-6490, 5pm-9pm daily May-Oct. and holidays, $10-23) is recommended. You'll enjoy elk meatballs in red wine and mushroom sauce, or pork loin with Jack Daniels sauce. Local huckleberry pie is a wonderful seasonal treat.

**Beckie's** (Union Creek Resort, 56484 Rte. 62, 541/560-3565 or 866/560-3565, 8am-9pm daily Apr.-Oct., 8am-7pm Sun.-Thurs., 8am-8pm Fri.-Sat. Nov.-Mar., $5-16) is a cozy place to stop for a bite to eat. One half of the building is an old log cabin; the other half is of modern design with plenty of windows. Breakfast comes with all the trimmings. The lunch menu features sandwiches and burgers. Dinner includes chicken, pork chops, and steak entrées.

# Klamath Falls

Klamath Falls, or "K Falls" as locals call it, is the population hub of south-central Oregon with about 20,000 people within the city limits and an additional 40,000 in the surrounding area. This community is used to hard times after witnessing the decline of its previous economic engines, starting with the railroads and moving on to the timber industry. Farming and ranching are still an important part of the local economy, as are tourism and the influx of new settlers, particularly retirees. The cost of living here is comparatively low, and the climate is dry, with more than 290 days of sunshine; winters are cool but not damp, and it's less cold and rainy than Bend.

Downtown Klamath Falls has a clutch of handsome historic buildings, many revitalized with interesting shops and dining spots, and three intriguing museums that shed light on different aspects of local history and culture. But the real draw of Klamath Falls is out in the surrounding countryside. The native trout of Klamath Lake and the nearby Wood and Williamson Rivers are legendary, averaging 21 inches. There's world-class white-water rafting on the upper Klamath River, with several hair-raising rapids topping Class IV. But most of all it's the Klamath Basin national wildlife refuges, a complex of six lake and wetland units stretching into California, that draw visitors—and lots of birds—to the area. The refuges host some 50 nesting pairs of bald eagles, as well as more than 400 other bird species.

## SIGHTS

Klamath Falls's museums are within walking distance of each other, and the broad downtown streets deserve a stroll.

### ( Favell Museum

A fine collection of Native American artifacts and Western art is found at the **Favell Museum** (125 W. Main St., 541/882-9996, www.favellmuseum.org, 10:30am-4:30pm Tues.-Sat., $10 adults, $5 children ages 6-16, children under 6 free, $25 family). Here you'll find beautiful displays of Native American stonework, bone and shell work, beadwork, quilts, basketry, pottery, and Pacific Northwest coast carvings as well as a collection of over 60,000 mounted arrowheads. Another attraction is the collection of miniature working firearms, ranging from Gatling guns to inch-long Colt 45s, displayed in the museum's walk-in vault.

The museum also houses one of Oregon's best collections of Western art. The gift shop and art gallery specialize in limited edition prints and original Western art.

### Baldwin Hotel Museum

Travel back in time to the early 1900s thanks to the **Baldwin Hotel Museum** (31 Main St., 541/883-4207, 10am-4pm Wed.-Sat. Memorial Day-Labor Day), which is adorned with

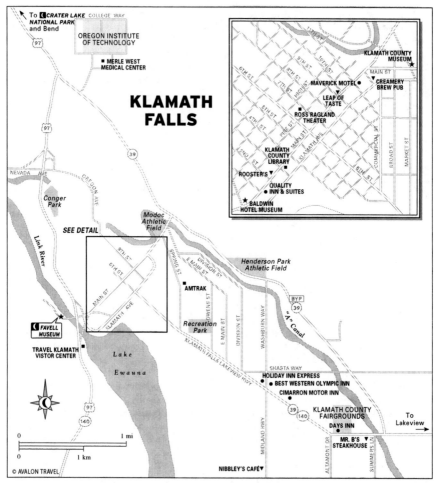

original fixtures and furnishings, the legacy of talented photographer Maud Baldwin. Her father—a U.S. senator—built the place first as a hardware store, then as a hotel. Presidents Teddy Roosevelt, Taft, and Wilson have all stayed here. Two different tours are offered: a two-hour tour of all four floors ($10 adults, $8 seniors and children ages 5-12), and a one-hour tour that visits just two floors ($5 adults, $4 seniors and children). The final full tour starts at 1:30pm, and the final shorter tour starts at 2:30pm.

## Klamath County Museum

You can get good background information on the region with a visit to the **Klamath County Museum** (1451 Main St., 541/883-4208, 9am-5pm Tues.-Sat., $5 adults, $4 seniors and students, $5 children ages 5-12) in the old national armory building. The natural history section has exhibits on fossils, geology, minerals, and indigenous wildlife of the Klamath Basin. The exploration and settlement area depicts the hardships of pioneer life, the events leading to

**The Klamath County Museum has good natural history exhibits.**

the Modoc Indian War, and events up through the world wars.

## Collier Memorial State Park

About 30 miles north of Klamath Falls on U.S. 97 is **Collier Memorial State Park** (541/783-2471 or 800/551-6949, day use free). Donated to the state in 1945 by Alfred and Andrew Collier as a memorial to their parents, this 146-acre park documents technological improvements in the history of logging.

The park's Pioneer Village includes a logger's homestead cabin stocked with a wide variety of tools and artifacts, a blacksmith shed, an assortment of logging machinery that includes log wagons with wheels made of cross-cut sections of logs bound in iron, and chain-drive trucks with hard rubber tires. Also on display are steam-propelled devices including tractors, a narrow-gauge locomotive, and a one-person handcart.

Don't miss the over-200-foot-long 16-foot-wide **Clatsop Fir,** a fallen tree that was mature when Columbus landed in the New

World. The tree could supply enough wood for several four-bedroom homes. For better or for worse, it's probably the largest Douglas fir ever cut.

## Wildlife Refuges

The lakes, marshes, and streams in the Klamath Basin are protected by six different wildlife refuges that stretch between southern Oregon and northern California and are centrally managed by the **Klamath Basin National Wildlife Refuge Complex.** The refuge complex headquarters and **visitor center** (530/667-2231, www.fws.gov/klamathbasinrefuges, 8am-4:30pm Mon.-Fri., 9am-4pm Sat.-Sun.) is 4 miles south of the California-Oregon border on U.S. 97.

December-February the Klamath Basin is home to one of the largest wintering concentration of bald eagles in the Lower 48 states. The thousands of winter waterfowl that reside here provide a plentiful food source for these raptors. By January, 700-800 eagles from as far north as southeastern Alaska's Chilkat River,

Saskatchewan, and the Northwest Territories congregate in the area.

In addition to a readily available food supply, the eagles require night-roosting areas. The **Bear Valley National Wildlife Refuge** (between Keno and Worden) has mature stands of timber that can support up to 300 eagles per night. The eagles prefer trees on northeastern slopes that protect them from the cold southwest and westerly winds. However, the eagles *don't* like it when people bother them. Hence the roosting areas are closed early November-March 30.

The good news is that there are still ample opportunities to view our national bird, especially when it is very cold. Contact the Fish and Wildlife office for the latest information on the best eagle-watching locations. Good sightings can be had driving to Bear Valley at sunrise. To get there, head 1 mile south of Worden on U.S. 97. Turn right on Keno Worden Road past the grain silos, cross the railroad tracks, and take an immediate left on the gravel road. Travel for about 1 mile and pull off the road. From here you can sometimes see up to 100 bald eagles soar from their roosts at the top of the ridge, headed to their daytime feeding area on the refuge to the east. Bring binoculars, warm clothing, and a camera with a telephoto lens.

A world-renowned event, the **Winter Wings Festival** (www.winterwingsfest.org) is held in February. The highlight is a predawn field trip to the nearby Bear Valley roost.

March-May is when waterfowl and shorebirds stop over in the basin on their way north to their breeding grounds in Alaska and Canada. They rest and fatten up during the spring to build the necessary strength and body fat to carry them through their long migration. May-July is the nesting season for thousands of marsh birds and waterfowl. The **Klamath Marsh National Wildlife Refuge** (north of Klamath Falls off U.S. 97) is a good place in spring to observe sandhill cranes, shorebirds, waterfowl, and raptors.

The summer months are ideal for taking the self-guided auto tour routes and canoe trails. Descriptive leaflets for both are available from the refuge office. Among the most prolific waterfowl and marsh bird areas in the Pacific Northwest, over 25,000 ducks, 2,600 Canada geese, and thousands of marsh and shorebirds are raised here each year. You may also see American white pelicans, *Pelecanus erythrorhynchos*, at the **Upper Klamath National Wildlife Refuge** (north of Klamath Falls) during the summer.

Another high point is the **Upper Klamath Canoe Trail,** which follows a 9.5-mile passage through lakes, marshes, and streams at the northwest corner of Upper Klamath Lake within the boundaries of the refuge. Birding is excellent along the canoe trail as mature ponderosa pines come right to the edge of the marsh, creating habitat for raptors, songbirds, and waterfowl. The trail departs from Rocky Point, about 25 miles northwest of Klamath Falls on Route 140. Canoe rentals ($40 per day) are available from **Rocky Point Resort** (28121 Rocky Point Rd., 541/356-2287, www.rockypointoregon.com).

**Tule Lake and Lower Klamath Refuges** (south of Klamath Falls in California) are open during daylight hours. Overnight camping is not permitted in any of the refuges.

## SPORTS AND RECREATION

With all the lakes, rivers, and mountains in the region, there's no shortage of fishing, rafting, golfing, and other recreational opportunities. Here's a short list of some local attractions.

### Boating

One way to get out onto Oregon's largest lake is to rent a sailboat through **Meridian Sail Center** (Pelican Marina, Dock C, 928 Front St., 541/884-5869, www.meridiansail.com). Sailboat rentals are $70-100 half-day, $100-140 full-day. Sailing instruction is also available. Call ahead for the sailing report and to make reservations.

### Fishing

Local guides can get you outfitted and on the water angling for the elusive big one. **Darren Roe Guide Service** (4849 Summers Ln., 541/884-3825, www.roeoutfitters.com) offers trips on Klamath Lake and the nearby Wood and Willamson Rivers, noted for their runs of wild trout. Rates are roughly $450 for two people for a full day.

### Golf

There are several area courses open to the public. **Harbor Links** (601 Harbor Isle Blvd., 541/882-0609) and **Shield Crest** (3151 Shieldcrest Dr., 541/884-1493) both offer 9- and 18-hole courses with greens fees in the $25-50 range. The **Running Y Ranch Resort** (5500 Running Y Rd., 541/850-5500 or 877/866-1266, www.runningy.com, $89-119 for 18 holes) offers a 7,138-yard 18-hole course designed by Arnold Palmer.

### Rafting

Twenty miles (just under an hour's drive) west of Klamath Falls is what's known as Hell's Corner of the Upper Klamath River. **Arrowhead River Adventures** (720 Greenleaf Dr., Eagle Point, 541/830-3388 or 800/227-7741, www.arrowheadadventures.com) offers daylong trips ($149) through this remote secluded canyon June-September. With several Class IV-plus rapids, the Upper Klamath provides some of the best spring and summer rafting in the state.

You can also arrange a raft trip in the Upper Klamath River canyons through Ashland's **Adventure Center** (40 N. Main St., Ashland, 541/488-2819 or 800/444-2819, www.rafting-tours.com). In addition to a day trip ($135, includes transportation to and from Ashland), they offer a two-day trip down the river with a night of fully catered riverside camping ($339).

## ENTERTAINMENT AND EVENTS

The region's cultural hub is the **Ross Ragland Theater** (218 N. 7th St., 541/884-5483, www.rrtheater.org). In addition to the Klamath Symphony and other community organizations, country stars, internationally acclaimed guest artists, and touring Broadway troupes grace the stage of this 800-seat auditorium. Call the theater or check the daily *Herald and News* to see what's scheduled.

## ACCOMMODATIONS

Travelers on a budget will appreciate **Maverick Motel** (1220 Main St., 541/882-6688 or 800/404-6690, www.maverickmotel.com, $50-55) and **Cimarron Motor Inn** (3060 S. 6th St., 541/882-4601 or 800/742-2648, www.cimarroninnklamathfalls.com, $65-89) for their pools and continental breakfasts, and for allowing pets.

Midrange properties are the domain of the chains. **Best Western Olympic Inn** (2627 S. 6th St., 541/882-9665, $119-149), **Holiday Inn Express** (2500 S. 6th St., 541/884-9999, $129-149), **Quality Inn** (100 Main St., 541/882-4666, $69-99), and **Days Inn** (3612 S. 6th St., 541/882-8864 or 800/329-7466, $69-79) all feature the expected pools, continental breakfasts, and other upgrades.

The **Running Y Ranch Resort** (5500 Running Y Rd., 541/850-5500 or 800/851-6013, www.runningy.com, $154-194 d hotel rooms) offers the total Klamath Basin package experience. This upscale golf resort has country club homes, and travelers can stay in the deluxe guest rooms at the ranch lodge. The 82 guest rooms are a mix of comfortable hotel-style rooms and well-appointed one-bedroom suites. Two- and three-bedroom houses are also available.

### Camping

Most of the campgrounds you'll find in the vicinity of Klamath Falls are privately owned RV campgrounds with electric, water, and sewer hookups as well as other creature comforts like swimming pools, laundries, and recreational halls. These properties also tend to be in prime locations, which accounts for rates that are steeper than those of their public counterparts. Fortunately, there are several places to pitch a tent in both types of park without having to deal with a 40-foot-long mobile home parked right next to your sleeping bag.

Across from the logging museum at **Collier Memorial State Park** is a pretty campground ($19-22), set near the convergence of the Williamson River (locally famous for its trout) and Spring Creek.

**Rocky Point Resort** (28121 Rocky Point Rd., 541/356-2287, www.rockypointoregon.com, Apr.-mid-Nov., tents $22, RVs $28-30, cabins $140) is close to the Upper Klamath National Wildlife Refuge, about a half-hour from Klamath Falls. This resort has 5 tent and 28 RV sites with hookups as well as rustic cabins. Flush toilets, showers, firewood, a laundry, a recreation hall, and other summer camp trappings are available. Ask about canoe rentals for trips on the Upper Klamath Canoe Trail.

Several other campgrounds are also found on Upper Klamath Lake. The best deal around is still **Hagelstein Park** (17301 Hwy. 97 N., 541/883-5371, Apr.-late Nov., free), a small park just off the highway with boat ramp. In addition to being the only campground on the east shore of the lake, it's the least expensive campground in the area. To get there, head north of Klamath Falls for 10 miles and look for signs on the right side of the road.

Approximately seven miles farther north on U.S. 97 is **KOA Klamath Falls** (3435 Shasta Way, 541/884-4644, year-round, $25-37, cabins $54). Set along the shore of Upper Klamath Lake, the park features 18 tent and 73 RV sites with hookups. In true KOA style, flush toilets, showers, a pool, a laundry, a recreation hall, and other amenities are available.

## FOOD

The popular spot for breakfast and lunch is **Nibbley's Cafe** (2650 Washburn Way, 541/883-2314, 6am-4pm Mon., 6am-9pm Tues.-Fri., 7am-9pm Sat., 8am-2pm Sun., breakfast $5-11). The oatmeal pancakes are locally renowned, and the omelets are yummy.

Right downtown **A Leap of Taste** (907 Main St., 541/850-9414, 7:30am-6pm Mon.-Fri., 8am-3pm Sat., $4-8) is a great place for a sandwich or coffee, but it's a bit more than that. It also stocks a small selection of organic groceries, including locally raised meat, and serves

as a place for young adults to learn job skills (in a way that's a bit more intentional than most coffee shops).

**Rooster's Steak and Chop House** (205 Main St., 541/850-8414, 4pm-10pm daily, $22-38) is K Falls's restaurant of the moment, with excellent steaks and a classy atmosphere.

A good spot for casual dining is the **Creamery Brew Pub & Grill** (1320 Main St., 541/273-5222, 11am-9:30pm daily, $8-18), with good beer and serviceable pub food. One of the great attractions of the Creamery is its outdoor seating on the building's old loading dock.

## INFORMATION

Over 2.2 million acres of Klamath County is publicly owned. The **Klamath Falls Ranger District Office** (2819 Dahlia St., 541/883-6714) can provide outdoor recreational information on the Winema National Forest and other surrounding natural areas. The **Bureau of Land Management** (2795 Anderson Ave., 541/883-6916) can also provide relevant information.

You'll find the **Oregon Welcome Center** on U.S. 97 about halfway between Klamath Falls and the California-Oregon border. They have a broad collection of brochures and information about locales all over the state.

For information on Klamath Falls, contact **Discover Klamath** (205 Riverside Dr., 541/882-1501 or 800/445-6728, www.discoverklamath.com).

## GETTING THERE

**Amtrak** (1600 Oak Ave., 541/884-2822) can connect you with northern and southern destinations via the *Coast Starlight* train. **Greyhound** (445 S. Spring St., 541/883-2609) can take you to Bend or the I-5 corridor. The **Point** bus (541/883-2609, www.oregon-point.com) provides connections to Ashland and Brookings.

# MAP SYMBOLS

| | | | |
|---|---|---|---|
| Expressway | ⬛ Highlight | ✗ Airfield | ⚲ Golf Course |
| Primary Road | ○ City/Town | ✗ Airport | ⓟ Parking Area |
| Secondary Road | ⊙ State Capital | ▲ Mountain | ▲ Archaeological Site |
| Unpaved Road | ⊛ National Capital | ✛ Unique Natural Feature | ⬥ Church |
| Trail | ★ Point of Interest | | ⬛ Gas Station |
| Ferry | ● Accommodation | Waterfall | Glacier |
| Railroad | ▼ Restaurant/Bar | ▲ Park | Mangrove |
| Pedestrian Walkway | ▪ Other Location | ⬛ Trailhead | Reef |
| Stairs | Λ Campground | Skiing Area | Swamp |

# CONVERSION TABLES

°C = (°F − 32) / 1.8
°F = (°C x 1.8) + 32
1 inch = 2.54 centimeters (cm)
1 foot = 0.304 meters (m)
1 yard = 0.914 meters
1 mile = 1.6093 kilometers (km)
1 km = 0.6214 miles
1 fathom = 1.8288 m
1 chain = 20.1168 m
1 furlong = 201.168 m
1 acre = 0.4047 hectares
1 sq km = 100 hectares
1 sq mile = 2.59 square km
1 ounce = 28.35 grams
1 pound = 0.4536 kilograms
1 short ton = 0.90718 metric ton
1 short ton = 2,000 pounds
1 long ton = 1.016 metric tons
1 long ton = 2,240 pounds
1 metric ton = 1,000 kilograms
1 quart = 0.94635 liters
1 US gallon = 3.7854 liters
1 Imperial gallon = 4.5459 liters
1 nautical mile = 1.852 km

**MOON SPOTLIGHT ASHLAND
& SOUTHERN OREGON**
Avalon Travel
a member of the Perseus Books Group
1700 Fourth Street
Berkeley, CA 94710, USA
www.moon.com

Editor: Leah Gordon
Series Manager: Kathryn Ettinger
Copy Editor: Ashley Benning
Graphics and Production Coordinator: Lucie Ericksen
Cover Design: Kathryn Osgood
Map Editor: Albert Angulo
Cartographers: Stephanie Poulain and Brian Shotwell

ISBN-13: 978-1-61238-791-8

Text © 2014 by W. C. McRae and Judy Jewell.
Maps © 2014 by Avalon Travel.
All rights reserved.

Front cover photo: Oregon Shakespeare Festival,
Henry VIII (2009): Ensemble © Jenny Graham
Title page photo: Emigrant Lake © Judy Jewell

Printed in the United States of America

All recommendations, including those for sights,
activities, hotels, restaurants, and shops, are based
on each author's individual judgment. We do not
accept payment for inclusion in our travel guides,
and our authors don't accept free goods or services
in exchange for positive coverage.

Although every effort was made to ensure that
the information was correct at the time of going
to press, the author and publisher do not assume
and hereby disclaim any liability to any party for any
loss or damage caused by errors, omissions, or any
potential travel disruption due to labor or financial
difficulty, whether such errors or omissions result
from negligence, accident, or any other cause.

# ABOUT THE AUTHORS

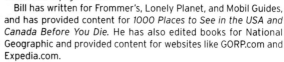

## Judy Jewell and W. C. McRae

Between the two of them, Judy Jewell and Bill McRae have lived in and traveled around Oregon for more than 50 years. During this time, they've also strayed out of state to research and write Moon Handbooks to Montana, Utah, and southern Utah's national parks (a.k.a. Zion and Bryce).

Judy graduated from Reed College and worked at Portland's renowned Powell's Books for 14 years as a book buyer and manager, until she decided to leave to write travel books. When she's not traveling around the West, she works as a technical and scientific editor and a yoga teacher.

Bill has written for Frommer's, Lonely Planet, and Mobil Guides, and has provided content for *1000 Places to See in the USA and Canada Before You Die*. He has also edited books for National Geographic and provided content for websites like GORP.com and Expedia.com.

Judy and Bill both live in Portland, Oregon.

© JOCELYN BOWIE

© ERICA SCHROEDER

CPSIA information can be obtained at www.ICGtesting.com
Printed in the USA
LVOW12s1232110614

389576LV00004BA/13/P